FOR
BETTER
FOR
WORSE

SHOULD I GET MARRIED?

If you marry, you will regret it; if you do not marry, you will also regret it; if you marry or do not marry, you will regret both. Laugh at the world's follies, you will regret it, weep over them, you will also regret that; laugh at the world's follies or weep over them, you will regret both; whether you laugh at the world's follies or weep over them, you will regret both. Believe a woman, you will regret it, believe her not, you will also regret that; believe a woman or believe her not, you will regret both; whether you believe a woman or believe her not, you will regret both. Hang yourself, you will regret it; do not hang yourself, and you will also regret that; hang yourself or do not hang yourself, you will regret both; whether you hang yourself or do not hang yourself, you will regret both. This, gentlemen, is the sum and substance of all philosophy

—Søren Kierkegaard, *Either/Or*

FOR
BETTER
FOR
WORSE

SHOULD I GET MARRIED?

NEEL BURTON

A

Acheron Press

Flectere si nequeo superos
Acheronta movebo

© Acheron Press 2017

Published by Acheron Press

A CIP catalogue record for this book is available from the British Library.

ISBN 978 0 9929127 7 2

Typeset by Phoenix Photosetting, Chatham, Kent, United Kingdom
Printed and bound by SRP Limited, Exeter, Devon, United Kingdom

About Neel Burton

Dr Neel Burton is a psychiatrist, philosopher, writer, and wine-lover who lives and teaches in Oxford, England.

He is a Fellow of Green-Templeton College, Oxford, and the recipient of the Society of Authors' Richard Asher Prize, the British Medical Association's Young Authors' Award, the Medical Journalists' Association Open Book Award, and a Best in the World Gourmand Drinks Award.

His work has been translated into several languages, including Chinese, Japanese, German, Italian, and Portuguese.

www.neelburton.com

Contents

Contents

Preface

Marriage is an ancient institution that evolved in a historical context of agrarian societies with low life expectancy, high fertility and infant mortality, and marked gender disparity. If it did serve our ancestors well, has it now outlived its usefulness? Whatever the answer to that question, there is nothing natural or pre-ordained about marriage, and while it may be suited to some, it cannot be suited to all.

This book, born out of a series of articles for *Psychology Today*, is intended as a thinking person's guide to marriage and its alternatives. It is not intended as a polemic, in one way or the other, and tries in as far as possible to let the facts and arguments speak for themselves—even though, in the final reckoning, marriage, like love, or trust, or religious belief, is, as it must be, an act of faith that transcends reason and prudence.

If bias has entered into this book, it has mostly been in the selection of topics. Some topics such as romantic love and the family are central to any discussion of marriage; but others such as the psychology of the orgy and the philosophy of forgiveness I have chosen because they are rarely discussed or because I felt

I might have something interesting or useful to contribute. The chapters on the history of kissing, the philosophy of lust, and loneliness/solitude are adapted from *Heaven and Hell* (2015) and the chapter on the psychology of love is adapted from *Hide and Seek* (2012). I have not specifically discussed the legal advantages and disadvantages of marriage because these vary from one jurisdiction to another, and according to individual circumstances such as the tax bracket of each of the spouses. There is a loose progression to the chapters, but each one is fairly self-contained and the reader may choose to dip in and out and progress in any order or none at all.

I really enjoyed writing this book, travelling in time and place and in the mind, and I hope that some of that enthusiasm can rub off on the reader.

Neel Burton
Oxford, September 2017

1

Monogamy

In the state of nature, people were generally polygamous, as are most animals. With many animals, the male leaves the female soon after mating and long before any offspring are born. A male bear will kill and sometimes eat any bear cub that it encounters, even if it is his own. On the other hand, over 90 per cent of avian species are socially monogamous, as are the emperor penguin, the prairie vole, and the red-backed salamander. The parasitic flatworm *Schistosoma mansoni*, one of the major agents of the disease schistosomiasis (bilharzia), is monogamous in its female-male pairings within the human body, suggesting that monogamy is not necessarily more sophisticated than polygamy. Can you feel the love blossoming inside you?

According to genetic studies, it is only relatively recently, about 10,000 years ago, that monogamy began to prevail over polygamy in human populations. Monogamous unions may have developed in tandem with sedentary agriculture, helping to preserve land and property within the same narrow kin group. Polygamy may enable a man to sire more offspring, but monogamy can, in certain circumstances, represent a more successful overall reproductive strategy. For example, by guarding a single female, a male can ensure that the female's offspring are also his, and prevent the infants from being killed by male rivals intent on returning the female to fertility. Compared to the young of other species, children are much more dependent, and for much longer. Bi-parental care makes them more likely to reach reproductive maturity. Without bi-parental care, human beings may never have evolved the large and hungry brains that have led to democracy, space exploration, and the Daily Mail.

A cuckold is a man who is unwittingly investing parental effort into offspring that are not genetically his own. There is an urban myth that 10–30 per cent of fathers are cuckolds, but a recent paper concluded on the basis of genetic studies that human extra-pair paternity rates 'have stayed near constant at around 1 per cent across several human societies over the past several hundred years'. Despite the potential genetic advantage to the offspring, cuckolding seems to have been kept in check by spousal jealousy and social and religious codes that discourage adultery, and by the fear of spousal aggression or desertion. A cuckold is sometimes represented with horns in an allusion to the mating habits of stags, which forfeit their mates when defeated by another male. Remember those school photos?

There are several instances of polygamy in the Old Testament: Moses had two wives, Abraham three, Jacob four, David at least 18, and Solomon all of 700. But biblical polygamy usually had a bitter ending. According to the Book of Kings, Solomon had 'seven hundred wives, princesses, and three hundred concubines', but 'his wives turned away his heart after other gods: and his heart was not perfect with the Lord his God…' The Old Testament Book of Deuteronomy favours the first wife in stating that a man must bequeath his property to his first-born son even if he hates that son's mother and loves another wife.

The creation story on the very first pages of the Bible clearly seeks to enforce a monogamous ethos. In Genesis 1, God seems to have created man and woman at the same time: 'So God created man in his own image, in the image of God created he him; male and female created he them.' After blessing them, the first thing God tells them is to 'be fruitful and multiply, and replenish the earth'. However, Genesis 2 finds Adam alone in Eden. God says that 'it is not good that the man should be alone', and creates Eve from one of Adam's ribs. Upon seeing Eve for the first time, Adam says: "This is now bone of my bones, and flesh of my flesh... Therefore shall a man leave his father and his mother, and shall cleave unto his wife: and they shall be one flesh." The serpent that draws Eve, and by Eve Adam, to eat from the tree of the knowledge of good and evil is ssseductive, and phallic in form, and may represent sexual temptation or adultery. To punish Eve, God curses her to the pangs of childbirth and to marital subservience.

Adam's pronouncement upon seeing Eve for the first time seems to imply marriage and monogamy as the norm for man. In his First Epistle to Timothy, Paul the Apostle (AD 5–67) declared that 'A bishop must be blameless, the husband of one wife...' The Roman Catholic Church has long condemned polygamy, arguing, albeit tautologically, that conjugal love must be undivided. But in a letter to the Saxon Chancellor Gregor Brück, the theologian and Protestant reformer Martin Luther (1483–1546) confided that he could not 'forbid a man to marry several wives, for it does not contradict scripture'—which technically it doesn't.

2

Polygamy

Historically, most cultures that permitted polygamy permitted polygyny (a man taking two or more wives) rather than polyandry (a woman taking two or more husbands). In the *Gallic War*, Julius Caesar claims that, among ancient Britons, 'ten and even twelve men have wives in common', particularly brothers, he says, or fathers and sons—which to me sounds more like group marriage than polyandry proper.

Polyandry is typically tied to scarcity of land and resources, as, for example, in certain parts of the Himalayas, and serves to limit population growth. If it involves several brothers married to one wife (fraternal polyandry), it also protects the family's land from division. In Europe, this was generally achieved through the feudal rule of primogeniture ('first born'), by which the eldest legitimate son inherited the entire estate of both his parents. Primogeniture has antecedents in the Bible, with, for example, Esau selling his 'birthright' to his younger brother Jacob.

Today, most countries that permit polygamy—invariably in the form of polygyny—are countries with a Muslim majority or sizeable Muslim minority. In some countries, such as India, polygamy is legal only for Muslims. In others, such as Russia and South Africa, it is illegal but not criminalized.

Under Islamic marital jurisprudence, a man can take up to four wives, so long as he treats them all equally. While it is true that Islam permits polygyny, it does not require or impose it: marriage can only occur by mutual consent, and a bride can stipulate that her husband-to-be not take a second wife. Monogamy is by far the norm in Muslim societies, as most men cannot afford to maintain more than one family, and many of those who can would rather do without the trouble.

Polygamy is illegal and criminalized across Europe and the Americas, in China, Australia, and other countries. Even so, there are many instances of polygamy in the West, especially within immigrant communities and certain religious groups such as the Fundamentalist Church of Jesus Christ of Latter-Day Saints (FLDS Church) and other Mormon fundamentalists.

A man who takes more than one wife satisfies some of his sexual urges, signals his high social status, and generally feels happier about himself. His many children supply him with a ready source of labour, and the means, through arranged marriages, to forge multiple social, economic, and political alliances. Polygyny may be costly, but in the long term it can make a rich man richer.

Even in monogamous societies, powerful men often establish long-term sexual relationships with women other than their wives (concubinage), although in this case the junior partners and the children born to them do not enjoy the same legal protections as the 'legitimate' wife and children. In some cases, a man might get divorced to marry a much younger woman (serial monogamy), thereby monopolizing the reproductive lifespan of more than one woman without suffering the social stigma of polygamy.

Polygyny might even benefit the women involved, who may come to enjoy one another's company and share out the burdens of housekeeping and childrearing. Younger wives may add to the social standing of the first wife, while at the same time subtracting from her workload. In times of war, with high male absenteeism and mortality, polygyny supports population growth and replenishment by ensuring that every female can find a mate.

Polygyny also has many drawbacks, particularly when seen through a modern, western lens. First and foremost, polygyny sanctions and perpetuates gender inequality, with co-wives officially and patently subordinated to their husband. Women in polygynous unions tend to marry at a younger age, into a setup that, by its very nature, fosters jealousy, competition, and conflict. Although the husband ought in principle to treat his co-wives equally, in practice he will almost inevitably favour one over the others—most likely the youngest, most recent one. Tensions may be reduced by establishing a clear hierarchy among the co-wives, or if the co-wives are sisters (sororal polygyny), or if they each keep a separate household (hut polygyny).

While polygyny may benefit the men involved, it denies wives to other men, especially young, low-status men, who, like all men, tend to measure their success by their manhood, that is, by the twin parameters of social status and fertility. With little to lose, these frustrated men are much more likely to turn to crime, including sexual violence.

Polygyny may also disadvantage the offspring, who receive a divided share of their father's attentions, which may be directed at his latest wife, or at amassing resources for his next one. On the other hand, the offspring share in the genes of an alpha male, and stand to benefit from his protection, resources, influence, outlook, and expertise.

3

Gender fluidity in gods and heroes

We have so far assumed that the sexes are neatly divided, but this is not the case, and certainly not with the gods. Many cultures have gods, demi-gods, and heroes with both male and female attributes. In Hindu mythology, Shiva is seduced by Vishnu's female avatar, Mohini, giving birth to the god Shasta (or Ayyappa). Shiva himself is often represented as Ardhanarishvara, an androgynous composite of Shiva and Parvati with a body that is male on the right-hand side and female on the left. Arjuna, the great warrior of the *Mahabharata* epic, spent a year as a woman, during which he took the name of Brihannala and taught song and dance to the princess Uttara.

The Mesopotamian Ishtar, the beautiful goddess of fertility, love, war, and sex, is sometimes represented with a beard to emphasize her more bellicose side. She could change a man into a woman, and the *assinnu*, *kurgarru*, and *kuku'u* who performed her cult had both male and female features. After the hero Gilgamesh rejected her offer of marriage, Ishtar unleashed the Bull of Heaven, ultimately leading to the death of Enkidu, whom Gilgamesh loved more than anyone: "Hear me, great ones of Uruk/ I weep for Enkidu, my friend/ Bitterly mourning like a woman mourning."

Hapi, the Egyptian god of the annual flooding of the Nile, brought such fertility as to be regarded by some as the father of the gods: he is generally depicted as intersex, with pendulous breasts and a ceremonial false beard. Hapi might be compared to Tlazolteotl, the Aztec goddess of fertility and sexuality. Tlazolteotl is associated with the moon, and, like the moon in that culture, has both male and female characteristics. Tlazolteotl is nothing if not complex and paradoxical: although she inspires vice, as Tlaelcuani the 'Eater of Filth' she is also able, not unlike Jesus, to purify us by absorbing our sins.

To seduce the nymph Callisto, Zeus, the king of the Greek gods, took the form of the goddess Artemis. Zeus took many lovers, but, as Xenophon points out, the only one to be granted immortality was the Trojan prince Ganymede. Other instances of same-sex love in Greek myth include: Apollo and Hyacinthus, Hermes and Krokus, Dionysus and Ampelos, Poseidon and Pelops, Orpheus and Kalais, and Heracles and Abderus, Hylas, and Iolaus.

The prophet Teiresias spent seven years as a woman, even giving birth to children in that time. One day, Zeus and his wife Hera dragged him into an argument about who has more pleasure in sex: woman, as Zeus claimed; or, as Hera claimed, man. Teiresias averred that, "Of ten parts a man enjoys only one." For this, Hera struck him blind, but Zeus compensated him with the gift of foresight and a lifespan of seven lives.

How might all this gender fluidity be interpreted? The union of masculine and feminine elements shows them to be complementary, inseparable, or one and the same, while emphasizing divine attributes such as power, creativity/fertility, and boundlessness. In its completeness, the union of the sexes also represents perfection and self-sufficiency, and, by extension, peace or even ecstasy. Spiritual schools tend to look favourably upon sexlessness, especially in the priestly caste, since the attraction between man and woman—or indeed between anyone and anyone—gives rise to worldly concerns and attachments, such as children and a home, and jealousy and heartbreak, which can detract from spiritual work and the liberation at which it aims. In heroes, gender fluidity may mark out the hero as more than a mere mortal. It may also, like the journey into the underworld, symbolize the search for knowledge, and in particular self-knowledge, that is the hallmark of the heroic quest.

4

Gender variation and same-sex relations in precolonial peoples

From Alaska to Patagonia, Native American cultures often held gender variant individuals in high regard, valuing them for their unique spiritual and artistic aptitudes and important economic and social contributions. Having been blessed with the spirits of both man and woman, these 'two-spirits', as they are still called, could mediate between men and women, and between this world and the other. They could accomplish the work of both sexes, meeting the need of the moment and compensating for any gender imbalances in their family or tribe. They often served as educators or guardians, taking in orphans or children from large or problem families.

European colonists saw two-spirits as 'sodomites', and, in 1513, the conquistador Vasco Nunez de Balboa infamously fed forty of them to his dogs. Unlike Europeans, who thought in fixed and binary terms, Native Americans understood gender as a continuum and sexuality as fluid. Neither did they confound gender and sexuality. Two-spirits were often males who preferred males, and sometimes even married a male, but they could also be males who preferred females, females who preferred males, and females who preferred females. This did not preclude them from sexual relations with the other gender, or make their same-sex partners into two-spirits.

In Samoa and the Samoan diaspora, *fa'afafine* ('in the manner of woman') are biological males who identify as third-gender. In most cases, boys are identified as fa'afafine from an early age, either because it is their natural inclination or because there are not enough girls in the family. To varying degrees, they take on the dress, manners, and responsibilities of a woman, although, if the need arises, they can also do the work of a man. Rather than being stigmatized, they are seen as special and gifted, and valued for their work ethic and commitment to family and community. Samoan culture does not recognize homosexuality as such: fa'afafine have sexual relations with men, although not other fa'afafine, and sometimes with women as well. The Samoan Fa'afafine Association organizes the Miss Fa'afafine pageant to fund community work and raise awareness of human rights. A third-gender role is also recognized in other Pacific Island cultures, with, among others, the *fiafifine* in Niue, the *fakaleiti* in Tonga, the *vaka sa lewa lewa* in Fiji, the *whakawahine* in New Zealand, the *rae rae* in Tahiti, and the *mahu* in Hawaii.

In Hawaiian culture, an *aikane* was a male friend of a chief, with whom he had sexual relations. Most aikanes were young males, although some had their own families. They had significant clout, and played an important part in the 1779 killing of Captain Cook at Kealakekua Bay. David Samwell, a Welsh surgeon on board Cook's ship, wrote of the aikane that it is their business 'to commit the Sin of Onan (masturbation) upon the old king... it is an office that is esteemed honourable among them and they have frequently asked us on seeing a handsome young fellow if he was not an Ikany (*sic*) to some of us'.

A common belief in Africa is that homosexuality is 'un-African', a 'white disease' brought across by Europeans. But, on the contrary, colonialists used the homosexuality that they found already in Africa as one more pretext for subjugating and Christianizing the continent. Many traditional African languages have very old words for gender variation and same-sex relations. More than two thousand years ago in what is now Zimbabwe, San Bushmen painted rocks with images of sexual congress between men. The Elizabethan traveller Andrew Battell, who lived among the Imbangala in what is now Angola, reported that the Imbangala 'are beastly in their living, for they have men in women's apparel, whom they keepe among their wives'. Battell also made mention of 'women witches … [who] use unlawfull lusts betweene themselves in mutuall filthinesse'. The Zande people of North Central Africa had a custom similar to the pederasty of Ancient Greece: a warrior would take on a younger male lover, who would, upon becoming a warrior, take on a younger male lover of his own. In the late 19th century, under the influence of British missionaries, some of the male pages in the court of King Mwanga II of Buganda (Uganda) converted to Christianity. Mwanga II had 16 wives, but when the pages began to refuse him sexual favours, he had them burnt at the stake. These are just a few among countless examples of culturally sanctioned 'homosexual' practices in Africa.

Today, homosexuality remains illegal in many African countries, in some cases punishable with life imprisonment or even death. In 2013, President Robert Mugabe of Zimbabwe described homosexuals as 'worse than pigs, goats and birds': "If you take men and lock them in a house for five years and tell them to come up with two children and they fail to do that, then we will chop off their heads." In 2015, President Yahya Jammeh of Gambia declared: "If you do it [in Gambia] I will slit your throat—if you are a man and want to marry another man in this country and we catch you, no one will ever set eyes on you again, and no white person can do anything about it." Unfortunately, scapegoating homosexuals by speaking and legislating against them pays dividends at the ballot box, and life for lesbian, gay, bisexual, and transgender people in many parts of Africa has been going from bad to worse. In 2015, President Obama made an impassioned speech on Kenyan soil, comparing homophobia to racial discrimination and warning President Uhuru Kenyatta that, "When you start treating people differently, because they're different … freedoms begin to erode. And bad things happen." Kenyatta curtly replied, "There are some things that we must admit we don't share."

This brief and incomplete survey suggests that gender variation and same-sex relations, though often driven underground, or omitted from the historical record, are timeless and universal, and part and parcel of the human condition. It also suggests that concepts of gender and sexuality are, to a large extent, culturally conditioned, and that our rigid and binary concepts of male and female and heterosexual and homosexual are not necessarily the historical norm, or the best way of apprehending, supporting, and celebrating the diversity, even within a single person, of human gender and sexuality.

5

Marriage in Ancient Egypt

A ttitudes to love, sex, and marriage in Ancient Egypt are
significant in themselves, and because they may have
informed or influenced mores and practices in Ancient Israel
(and therefore in the Bible) and as far out as Ancient Greece
and Ancient Rome. According to the Book of Exodus, Pharaoh
gave the order for every son born to the Hebrews to be drowned
because he feared being deposed by their growing number—which
is how baby Moses ended up in an ark of bulrushes on the Nile, to
be rescued by Pharaoh's daughter. The Ancient Greek philosopher
Thales of Miletus, whom Plato (428/427–348/347 BC) regarded
as one of the seven sages of Greece, received instruction from
Egyptian priests, and, while in Egypt, determined the height of
the pyramids by measuring their shadows at the time of day when
his own shadow was as long as he was tall. Plato himself travelled
to Egypt, and, according to Plutarch, funded his voyage by selling
Attic olive oil to the Egyptians.

We do not have a complete picture of marriage in Ancient Egypt.
The period spans almost 3,000 years, from 3,100 BC to 332 BC, and
attitudes may have varied quite considerably across the centuries,
or even from one ruler to the next. It seems that men and women

were almost equal in status, with the women enjoying more rights, such as the right to dispose of property or initiate divorce, than they would have in Ancient Athens or Ancient Rome. In the art of the period, women are often depicted supporting or clasping their husband, and husband and wife referred to each other as 'brother' or 'sister', again, suggesting a relationship of equals or near-equals.

The Egyptians enjoyed sensuous pleasures and, although proper, they were not in the least prudish. Their myths are replete with all kinds of sex. They represented the cosmos with Nut, goddess of the night sky, overarching her ithyphallic (erect) brother Geb, god of the earth. They attached false penises to male mummies and false nipples to female ones, to equip the dead for sex in the afterlife. They did not value chastity, with no word for 'virginity', and illegitimacy carried neither shame nor stigma. The Ebers medical papyrus, which dates back to the middle of the second millennium BC, contains a recipe for a contraceptive pessary, failing which it was possible to contract an abortion. Adultery on the other hand was a definite taboo, especially on the part of the wife, and women who strayed out of the marriage bed could be severely punished, including by mutilation, stoning, or burning at the stake.

In general, people sought to marry within their social class, but had little regard for race or even nationality. They sometimes married a cousin but, except for royals, steered clear from anything closer than a first cousin. Men usually got married at about 16–20 years old, or as soon as they had picked up a trade from which to support a wife and eventual children. Women usually got married at a younger age, at around 13 years old, or just after puberty, and it was not uncommon for an old man (old by the standards of the day) to marry a pubertal girl.

Marriage was usually contracted between the groom and the bride's parents, with the groom or his family offering money or gifts to seal the deal and compensate the bride's family for the loss of a daughter. An agreement was drawn up at the start of marriage to provide for the woman and eventual children in case of divorce, and the items that a woman brought into marriage remained her own. Marriage may have been marked by a celebration, but there was no wedding ritual as such. As soon as the bride moved her belongings into the groom's house, they were considered married. In some cases, a couple entered into a trial marriage lasting for one year, a so-called 'year of eating', after which the marriage could be either progressed or annulled.

Divorce was straightforward. Husband or wife could get divorced simply by saying so, even if they had no specific grounds such as adultery or infertility. Unlike in Ancient Athens and Ancient Rome, the children of the marriage belonged to the mother, and followed after her. The man paid alimony to the woman, whether or not they had children, until and unless she took another husband. There was no stigma attached to divorce, and divorcees could easily remarry, although such was the emphasis on having children that a woman much beyond the peak of her fertility would have had difficulty in finding a new husband. Despite the relative ease of divorce, people worked hard at their marriages, not least because they believed that it would last for all eternity, with a departed wife able to torment an inequitable husband from beyond the grave. The Egyptians held that, after death, they would stand in judgement before the god Osiris, who, they hoped, would allow them passage into the Field of Reeds where they would be reunited with the people and possessions that they held dear.

Osiris had married his sister Isis, and royals often followed in that example, partly because they thought of themselves as divine and partly to legitimize their succession. Cleopatra the lover of Caesar and Mark Antony married both of her brothers, Ptolemy XIII and Ptolemy XIV. Some pharaohs even married their own daughters, although this may have been an honorary marriage to elevate the status of a princess. Unlike normal Egyptians, for whom it was forbidden, pharaohs often took several wives, enabling them to forge or strengthen domestic and international alliances. That said, one of the wives, often a sister or half-sister, would prime over the others and carry the title of Great Royal Wife. Tutankhamun, who reigned from 1332 to 1323 BC and suffered from numerous deformities, was the son of Akhenaten and one of Akhenaten's sisters. He took for wife his half-sister Ankhesenamun, daughter of Akhenaten and his Great Royal Wife Nefertiti. Before marrying Tutankhamun, Ankhesenamun had been married to her father Akhenaten. Tutankhamun and Ankhesenamun had two daughters, but both were stillborn owing, no doubt, to the high degree of inbreeding.

6

Three tales of same-sex love in Ancient Egypt

Primary sources from the period are largely silent on the subject of same-sex love, and the principal evidence, which is open to interpolation, comes from just three areas: a myth about the gods Horus and Seth, a historical tale about Pharaoh Neferkare and his general Sasenet, and the excavated tomb of court officials Nyankhkhnum and Khnumhotep.

In the *Contendings of Horus and Seth*, a mythological story that exists in several versions, Seth and his nephew Horus vie for the throne of Egypt. Seth insists on getting the better of Horus. At last, he decides to subjugate him by inebriating, seducing, and, at last, inseminating him. "How beautiful are your buttocks, how vital!" used by Seth on his nephew, is probably the oldest recorded chat-up line in history. In the event, Horus is not all that drunk, and succeeds in catching Seth's semen in his hand. The next day, he shows his manky hand to his mother Isis, and together they plot revenge. Horus masturbates into Seth's lunchtime lettuce. Having eaten of the salad and sauce, Seth puts his case before the tribunal of the gods, but Horus disputes his claims. When, at last, Thoth calls forth their semen, that of Seth rises from the Nile, while that of Horus pours out of Seth's mouth.

This myth suggests that, in Ancient Egypt as in Ancient Rome, the sticking point, if you'll forgive the pun, was not so much with same-sex love *per se* as with a male playing a passive or receptive role. In 46 BC, Caesar submitted, or appeared to have submitted, to Nicomedes IV of Bithynia, leading to the disparaging title, 'the Queen of Bithynia'. A popular quip at the time ran: *Gallias Caesar subegit, Caesarem Nicomedes* ('Caesar subjugated Gaul, and Nicomedes Caesar'). It is notable that Horus had no qualms with being seduced by Seth, or even with bedding him, but only with being inseminated by him.

From three extant fragments, it is possible to reconstruct the 23rd century BC story of Pharaoh Neferkare (the long-reigning Pepi II) and his clandestine nocturnal visits to General Sasenet. A spy observed Neferkare going on his own from the royal palace to Sasenet's house. Once there, 'he threw a brick after stamping with his foot. Then a ladder was lowered to him (and) he climbed up.' Neferkare spent four hours with Sasenet, leaving only 'after his majesty had done that which he had wanted to do with him'. One fragment specifies that there was no woman, or wife, in Sasenet's house, and the same incomplete sentence also contains the word 'love'. The spy confirms to himself that 'the rumours about [Neferkare] going out at night are true'. The tale is censorious of the king's conduct, but more because it does not befit a king and god than because it involves same-sex love.

In the 25th century BC, Nyankhkhnum and Khnumhotep shared the title of Overseer of the Manicurists at the court of Pharaoh

Nyuserre Ini. As with the Gentleman of the Bedchamber at the royal court of England, the title is much more prestigious than it sounds, since Nyankhkhnum and Khnumhotep would have been granted the rare privilege of touching the person of the pharaoh, and may have been his close confidants. When they died, Nyankhkhnum and Khnumhotep were buried together in a mastaba tomb. In this tomb, they are severally depicted embracing and, in one instance, even touching noses, which in Ancient Egypt generally signified kissing. As their wives and children also feature in the tomb, it has been suggested that they were brothers rather than lovers—but having a family need not have prevented them from being lovers, and in the tomb they are represented in the same manner as husband and wife. Nyankhkhnum and Khnumhotep may well be the oldest recorded same-sex couple in history.

Like all ancient peoples, the Egyptians valued fertility and dominance, and disapproved in particular of the passive or receptive male role. But they did not have a rigid convention of sexuality as either heterosexual or homosexual, and, at least at certain times, and in certain strata, may have tolerated and even celebrated same-sex love.

7

The history and psychology of the orgy

The Ancient Egyptian *Book of the Heavenly Cow* contains the Myth of the Destruction of Mankind. Displeased with the mounting rebelliousness of mankind, the ageing Sun God Ra sends his daughter Hathor to wreak revenge. Hathor takes the form of the bloodthirsty lioness Sekhmet and rampages up and down the Nile Valley, killing every man, woman, and child in sight. With mankind on the verge of extinction, Ra takes pity, and floods the fields with beer dyed red with ochre. Mistaking the beer for blood, Sekhmet drinks to intoxication and falls asleep—to arise in the benign form of Hathor, the goddess of joy, love, and fertility. To commemorate this event, the Ancient Egyptians held communal Festivals of Drunkenness at the beginning of their calendar in mid-August, when the Nile is swelling. Revellers drank to the point of passing out, to be awoken by the beating of drums, symbolizing the transformation of Sekhmet into Hathor. The revels, which had an important religious dimension and typically took place in temples and shrines, also included dancing and public sex, in part to imitate and propitiate the flood and fertility to come.

The word 'orgy', which ultimately derives from the Ancient Greek *orgion/orgia*, entered the English language in the 1560s to mean 'any licentious revelry'. Today, people think of an orgy as a party involving open and unrestrained sex between diverse people with no or little prior knowledge of one another. But originally, *orgia* referred to the secret rites of the Ancient Greek mystery cults such as the Dionysian Mysteries and the Cult of Cybele, which aimed above all at ecstatic union with the divine.

Dionysus, who, like Jesus, died and was reborn, was the god of wine, regeneration, fertility, theatre, and religious ecstasy, and was most fervently celebrated around the time of the vernal equinox. The procession begins at sunset, led by torchbearers and followed by wine and fruit bearers, musicians, and a throng of revellers wearing masks and, well, not much else. Closing the parade is a giant phallus representing the resurrection of the twice-born god. Everyone is pushing and shoving, singing and dancing, and shouting the name of the god stirred in with ribaldry and obscenity—giving rise to an early form of theatre and comedy. Having arrived at a clearing in the woods, the crowd goes wild with drinking, dancing, and every imaginable manner of sex. The god is in the wine, and to imbibe it is to be possessed by his spirit—although in the bull's horn the booze may have been interlaced with other entheogens (substances that 'generate the divine from within'). Animals, which stand in for the god, are hunted down, ripped apart with bare hands, and consumed raw with the blood still warm and dripping.

The 'Dionysian' impulse for irrationality and chaos can be understood as a natural inversion of, and release from, the habitual 'Apollonian' order and restraint imposed by the state and state

religion. In the *Birth of Tragedy* (1872), the German philosopher
Friedrich Nietzsche recognizes it as a primal and universal force:

> *Either through the influence of narcotic drink, of which all*
> *primitive men and peoples speak, or through the powerful coming*
> *on of spring, which drives joyfully through all of nature, that*
> *Dionysian excitement arises. As its power increases, the subjective*
> *fades into complete forgetfulness of self. In the German Middle*
> *Ages under the same power of Dionysus constantly growing hordes*
> *waltzed from place to place, singing and dancing. In that St. John's*
> *and St. Vitus's dancing we recognize the Bacchic chorus of the*
> *Greeks once again, and its precursors in Asia Minor, right back to*
> *Babylon and the orgiastic Sacaea.*

By diverting the Dionysian impulse into special rites on special
days, the orgy kept it under control, preventing it from surfacing
in more insidious and perfidious ways. More than that, it
transformed it into an invigorating and liberating—and, in that
much, profoundly religious—celebration of life and the life force.
It permitted people to escape from their artificial and restricted
social roles to regress into a more authentic state of nature,
which modern psychologists have associated with the Freudian
id or unconscious. It appealed most to marginal groups, since it
set aside the usual hierarchies of man over woman, master over
slave, patrician over commoner, rich over poor, and citizen over
foreigner. In short, it gave people a much-needed break—like
modern holidays, but cheaper and more effective.

The Dionysian cult spread through the Greek colonies to Rome.
In 186 BC, the Roman Senate severely restricted it through the
senatus consultum de Bacchanalibus ('senatorial decree concerning

the Bacchanalia')—which can still be read today. According to
the Roman historian Livy, the decree led to more executions
than imprisonments, with many committing suicide to avoid
indictment. Illicit Bacchanalia persisted, especially in Southern
Italy, but gradually folded into the much tamer Liberalia in honour
of Liber Pater ('Free Father'), the Roman god of wine and fertility
who so resembled Bacchus/Dionysus as, eventually, to merge
into him. Like the Dionysian cult, the Liberalia featured a giant
phallus, carted through the countryside to fertilize the land and
safeguard crops—after which a virtuous matron placed a wreath on
top of the phallus. 'Depravity' featured in many Roman religious
festivals such as the Floralia, with naked dancing prostitutes, and
the Lupercalia, with naked noblemen running through the streets
and whipping willing ladies with strips of goatskin.

The 4th century reign of Constantius II marked the beginning
of the formal persecution of paganism by the Christian Roman
Empire. But the springtime fertility orgy survived through the
centuries, albeit in attenuated forms. At last, unable to suppress it,
the Church integrated it into its calendar as Carnival, which, still
today, involves reversal of social norms and roles, licentiousness,
and feasting ahead of the deprivations of Lent. But one doesn't
have to wait for Carnival to have an orgy. In the summer of 2017,
as reported in the Italian and international press, the police broke
up a drug-fuelled gay orgy at the Vatican—the problem in this case
being with the drugs rather than the orgy *per se*.

May Day celebrations across Europe and North America trace
their origins to the Roman Floralia and corresponding Celtic
traditions. In mediaeval times, people danced around the gigantic
phallic symbol of the Maypole before descending into the fields or

woods for indiscriminate sex, supposedly to fertilize the land. In the *Anatomie of Abuses* (1583), the puritan Philip Stubbs inveighs against these traditions:

> *What clipping, what culling, what kissing and bussing, what smooching and slobbering one of another, what filthy groping and unclean handling is not practised in the dances … I have heard it creditably reported (and that* viva voce*) by men of great gravitie and reputation, that of fortie, threescore, or a hundred maides going to the wood over night, there have scaresly the third part of them returned home againe undefiled.*

In 1644, the Puritans outlawed Maypoles in England, with the Long Parliament's ordinance damning them as 'a Heathenish vanity, generally abused to superstition and wickedness'.

'Ecstasy' literally means 'to be or stand outside oneself'. It is a trance-like state in which consciousness of an object is so heightened that the subject dissolves or merges into the object. Albert Einstein called it the 'mystic emotion', and spoke of it as 'the finest emotion of which we are capable', 'the germ of all art and all true science', and 'the core of the true religious sentiment'. More than ever before, modern society emphasizes the sovereign supremacy of the ego and the ultimate separateness and responsibility of each and every one of us. From a young age, we are taught to remain in tight control of our ego or persona with the aim of projecting it as far out as possible. As a result, we have lost the art of letting go—and, indeed, no longer even recognize the possibility—leading to a poverty or monotony of conscious experience. Letting go can threaten the life that we have built or even the person that we have become, but it can also free us from our modern narrowness and neediness, and deliver, or re-deliver, us into a bigger and brighter world. Little children have a quiescent or merged ego, which is why they brim with joy and wonder. Youth and ecstasy are the echoes of a primordial wisdom.

8

Marriage in the Bible

Is the married life better than celibacy? What does the Bible say? Jesus did not marry, and neither did Paul the Apostle and most of the Prophets. In his First Letter to the Corinthians, St Paul clearly favours celibacy and chastity, but accepts that most people cannot 'abide even as I' and to them he advises that 'it is better to marry than to burn':

It is good for a man not to touch a woman. Nevertheless, to avoid fornication, let every man have his own wife, and let every woman have her own husband ... But I speak this by permission, and not of commandment. For I would that all men were even as I myself. But every man hath his proper gift of God, one after this manner, and another after that. I say therefore to the unmarried and widows, it is good for them if they abide even as I. But if they cannot contain, let them marry: for it is better to marry than to burn ... He that is unmarried careth for the things that belong to the Lord, how he may please the Lord: But he that is married careth for the things that are of the world, how he may please his wife.

While St Paul permits (but does not command) marriage, Solomon, the apocryphal author of Ecclesiastes, seems—despite, or because of, his 700 wives—to warn against it, as well as against lust, on the grounds that they remove from the path to God:

> *I applied mine heart to know, and to search, and to seek out wisdom, and the reason of things, and to know the wickedness of folly, even of foolishness and madness: And I find more bitter than death the woman, whose heart is snares and nets, and her hands as bands: whosoever pleaseth God shall escape her; but the sinner shall be taken by her.*

The early Church Fathers took their cue from Solomon and especially St Paul in favouring the freedom of celibacy over the bondage of marriage and family. Noting that the angels are single, St John Chrysostom argued that celibacy surpasses marriage inasmuch as angels exceed men. Writing in the third century, St Cyprian maintained that, although God had commanded Adam and Eve to multiply, the world, by now, was full. St Augustine (354–430) summed it all up rather neatly: 'Marriage and fornication are not evils, whereof the second is worse: but marriage and continence are two goods, whereof the second is better.'

From the Old Testament, it seems that marriages could be arranged, and that the virginity of the bride was paramount. In Genesis 24, Abraham makes his eldest servant swear to pick a wife for his son, not from the Canaanites but from his own kin, effectively arranging his son's marriage. According to Deuteronomy, if a newly wed bride is found not to have been a virgin, she should be stoned to death in front of the door to her father's house 'because she wrought folly in Israel, to play the whore in her father's house'.

Once married, should a wife be subservient? Used by God to introduce Eve in Genesis 2:18, the word 'help', 'helper', 'helpmeet', or 'helpmate', though possibly a mistranslation, suggests that Eve's subordination to Adam predated the fall and God's curse of marital subservience. According to St Peter, Sara obeyed her husband Abraham, 'calling him lord'. In his Letter to the Ephesians, St Paul compares marriage to the relation between Christ and the Church: 'Wives, submit yourselves unto your own husbands, as unto the Lord. For the husband is the head of the wife, even as Christ is the head of the Church … Therefore as the church is subject unto Christ, so let the wives be to their own husbands in every thing.' In his First Letter to the Corinthians, he establishes a clear chain of authority: 'But I would have you know that the head of every man is Christ; and the head of the woman is the man; and the head of Christ is God.'

In the Middle Ages, the word 'obey' was introduced into marriage vows. Even so, a wife's subjection to her husband is not understood to be unconditional. In his Letter to the Galatians, St Paul says that faith levels the field: 'But after the faith is come… There is neither Jew nor Greek, there is neither bond nor free, there is neither male nor female: for ye are all one in Christ Jesus.' In his encyclical Arcanum (1880) Pope Leo XIII states that, 'the woman… must be subject to her husband and obey him; not indeed, as a servant, but as a companion, so that her obedience shall be wanting in neither honour nor dignity.'

Is recreational sex permissible within marriage? For St Paul, lust should not form the basis of a marriage. But once married, sex should not be withheld: 'Let thy fountain be blessed: and rejoice with the wife of thy youth. Let her be as the loving hind and pleasant roe; let her breasts satisfy thee at all times; and be thou ravished always with her love' (Proverbs 5:18–19). St Paul seems to agree, albeit with less poetry: 'Let the husband render unto the wife due benevolence: and likewise also the wife unto the husband. The wife hath not power of her own body, but the husband; and likewise also the husband hath not power of his own body, but the wife.'

The practice of levirate marriage is set out in Deuteronomy 25. In essence, a childless widow shall not re-marry with a stranger, but with her late husband's brother; and their firstborn son shall succeed in the name and estate of the late husband. This could concern the said brother-in-law, who, by fathering a child in his brother's line, could be creating a claimant on the larger part of his inheritance. When God killed Er, Er's father Judah told his second son Onan to marry Er's widow Tamar and 'raise up seed' to his brother. But when he lied with Tamar, Onan, who 'knew that the seed should not be his', spilled his semen on the ground: 'And the thing which he did displeased the Lord, wherefore he slew him also.' This episode is largely responsible for the ban on contraception and masturbation.

Adultery is forbidden in several places. It is, of course, the subject of one of the Ten Commandments in Exodus 20. David famously lusted after the bathing Bathsheba and impregnated her, leading, ultimately, to the death of that child, the death of Bathsheba's husband Uriah the Hittite, and the revolt of David's son Absalom. St Paul inveighs against adultery in more than one place, and St Matthew goes so far as to equate it with a lustful thought: 'But I say unto you, that whosoever looketh on a woman to lust after her hath committed adultery with her already in his heart.' According to Deuteronomy, an illegitimate child and his descendants cannot be admitted into the Church: 'A bastard shall not enter into the congregation of the Lord; even to his tenth generation shall he not enter into the congregation of the Lord.'

In Old Testament times, a husband could easily divorce his wife—see, for example, Deuteronomy 24. Jesus, however, forbids it: 'But I say unto you, that whosoever shall put away his wife, saving for the cause of fornication (Gk. *porneia*), causeth her to commit adultery: and whosoever shall marry her that is divorced committeth adultery.' Jesus refers back to Genesis 1 and 2 when discussing the indissolubility of marriage:

> *Have ye not read, that He which made them at the beginning made them male and female, and said, for this cause shall a man leave father and mother, and shall cleave to his wife: and they twain shall be one flesh? Wherefore they are no more twain but one flesh. What therefore God hath joined together, let not man put asunder.*

By leaning upon Genesis 1, Jesus may be implying that marriage ought to be between a man and a woman. Jesus performed his first public miracle at the marriage at Cana, saving the day by turning water into wine. This story has been upheld as evidence that he supported marriage, and also as an argument against teetotalism!

9

Love in the Bible

The concept of romantic love, which, as we shall see, is fairly modern, barely exists in the Bible. All love is directed at God, and the love for the spouse and more generally for the other is subsumed under the love of God. In the Binding of Isaac, Abraham's love for God trumps his love for Isaac his own son, whom he is willing to sacrifice for no other reason than that God commanded it.

Today, the most popular reading for weddings is Chapter 13 of St Paul's First Letter to the Corinthians. Here is a quick run-through:

> *Love is patient; love is kind, love is not envious or boastful or arrogant or rude. It does not insist on its own way: it is not irritable or resentful; it does not rejoice in wrongdoing, but rejoices in the truth. It bears all things, believes all things, hopes all things, endures all things … When I was a child, I spoke like a child, I thought like a child, I reasoned like a child; when I became an adult, I put an end to childish ways … And now faith, hope, and love abide, these three, and the greatest of these is love.*

The problem in this context is that St Paul is not referring to bleary-eyed romantic love, but to Christian love for our fellow men. The New Revised Standard Version of the Bible, which is the source of the above passage, gives the Greek *agape* as 'love', but the King James Version—which I am generally quoting—prefers to render it as 'charity': 'And now abideth faith, hope, charity, these three; but the greatest of these is charity.' Faith, hope, and charity are called the three theological virtues—'theological' because they are born out of the grace of God, and because they have God for their object. Charity in particular is the love of man for God, and through God, for his fellow men.

Even the Song of Songs (or Song of Solomon), which appears to celebrate sexual love, is read by the Jewish tradition as an allegory of the relationship between God and Israel, and by the Christian tradition as an allegory of the relationship between Christ and his 'bride', the Christian Church. But it's pretty spicy stuff: 'I am the rose of Sharon, and the lily of the valleys. As the lily among thorns, so is my love among the daughters. As the apple tree among the trees of the wood, so is my beloved among the sons. I sat down under his shadow with great delight, and his fruit was sweet to my taste.'

So it is perhaps not entirely surprising that the two greatest love stories in the Bible are not of husband and wife, nor even of man and woman, but of man and man, and woman and woman. David rivalled Jonathan, son of King Saul, for the throne of Israel. After slaying Goliath, he appeared before Saul with Goliath's head in his hand: 'And it came to pass, when he had made an end of speaking unto Saul, that the soul of Jonathan was knit with the soul of David, and Jonathan loved him as his own soul … And Jonathan stripped himself of the robe that was upon him, and gave it to David, and his garments, even to his sword, and to his bow, and to his girdle.' One evening, Saul rebuked Jonathan for favouring David over his own father and family: 'Thou son of the perverse rebellious woman, do not I know that thou hast chosen the son of Jesse to thine own confusion, and unto the confusion of thy mother's nakedness?' Upon learning of Jonathan's death on Mount Gilboa, David lamented: 'I am distressed for thee, my brother Jonathan: very pleasant hast thou been unto me: thy love to me was wonderful, passing the love of women.' David and Jonathan both had wives and children, and we are to believe that the love they shared was homosocial rather than homosexual.

In the Book of Ruth, Naomi is married to Elimelech. A famine leads them and their two sons to move from Bethlehem to Moab. In time, Elimelech dies, as do their two sons, leaving Naomi and her two daughters in law destitute. Naomi returns to Bethlehem, entreating her daughters in law, who are Moabites and thus from a different ethnic group, not to follow in her barren footsteps. But Ruth insists upon accompanying her: "Intreat me not to leave thee, or to return from the following after thee: for whither thou goest, I will go; and where thou lodgest, I will lodge: thy people shall be my people, and thy God my God: Where thou diest, I will die, and there will be buried..." This sounds more like a wedding vow than anything I might say to a mother in law.

When the pair arrive in Bethlehem, Naomi tells the Bethlehemites: 'Do not call me Naomi, call me Mara ('Bitter'), for the Almighty has dealt very bitterly with me.' Ruth takes to gleaning in the barley fields of Boaz, who it transpires, is a kinsman of Elimelech, Naomi's late husband. With Naomi's encouragement, Ruth marries Boaz, who bears Ruth a son, Obed. Interestingly, it is as if Obed were the son of Naomi: 'And the women said unto Naomi, Blessed be the Lord, which hath not left thee this day without a kinsman, that his name may be famous in Israel. And he shall be unto thee a restorer of thy life, and a nourisher of thine old age, for thy daughter in law, which loveth thee, which is better to thee than seven sons, hath born him. And Naomi took the child, and laid it in her bosom, and became nurse unto it. And the women her neighbours gave it a name, saying, There is a son born to Naomi...'

For the genealogy, Obed was the father of Jesse, and through Jesse, the grandfather of David.

10

Same-sex relations in the Bible

The Book of Leviticus clearly condemns same-sex relations, as well as touching pork, eating shellfish, and getting a tattoo or a round haircut: 'Thou shalt not lie with mankind, as with womankind: it is abomination.' The punishment for those who engage in same-sex relations is harsh: 'they shall surely be put to death; their blood shall be upon them.' St Paul seems to echo Leviticus in condemning the 'abusers of themselves with mankind' and the 'soft' or 'effeminate', or again 'them that defile themselves with mankind'—although, given the original Greek, and the cultural context, it could be that he is simply speaking out against the male prostitution that he found all around him.

What of Sodom, destroyed by fire and brimstone? In Genesis 19, Lot gives shelter to two beautiful angels. The men of Sodom (or Sodomites) threaten to force themselves upon Lot's guests, and such is Lot's idea of hospitality that he offers up his virgin daughters in their stead: 'Behold now, I have two daughters which have not known man; let me, I pray you, bring them out unto you, and do ye to them as is good in your eyes: only unto these men do nothing; for therefore came they under the shadow of my roof.'

But it is not clear whether the sin of Sodom was same-sex rape, lack of hospitality, or both or other.

The only reference to same-sex love between women, as well as men, is in St Paul's First Letter to the Romans. To punish the people for their idolatry, 'God gave them up unto vile affections: for even their women did change the natural (Gr. *physikos*, 'produced by nature') use into that which is against nature: and likewise also the men, leaving the natural use of the woman, burned in their lust one toward another…' It could be that, rather than same-sex love, St Paul is in fact condemning the prostitution and pederasty of the Roman world; or, more specifically, the pagan practice of priests and priestesses prostituting themselves out of their temples; or else merely those people who go against their nature, that is, against their supposedly heterosexual orientation. Here again, his meaning is far from clear.

Despite David and Jonathan, and Ruth and Naomi, the concept of homosexuality as a sexual orientation is relatively recent. The only possible reference to homosexuality as a sexual orientation is in Matthew 19, when Jesus speaks of 'eunuchs which were so born from their mother's womb'.

To conclude on the last three 'biblical' chapters, many traditional attitudes have come down from the Bible. But the Bible is not only or even primarily an instruction manual. It is not a unified work. It often contradicts itself. It lends itself to interpretation. It is open to misinterpretation. Choices made in style and translation can reflect the times and prejudices of the translator. Still, for better or worse, no single book has exerted a greater influence on the way we think and live.

11

An interpretation of Adam and Eve

The first book of the Old Testament, Genesis, opens upon the story of Adam and Eve. According to a poll carried out in 2014 for the Biologos Foundation, more than half of Americans believe that 'Adam and Eve were real people'. Whether literal or allegorical, what is the significance, and legacy, of their story?

Man

On the sixth day, after having created everything else, God fashioned man out of the dust of the ground, and breathed into his nostrils the breath of life. 'And so God created man in his image, in the image of God created he him; male and female created he them.' He gave them dominion over the animals, and told them to subdue and replenish the earth.

In Genesis 1, it seems that God created man and woman at the same time. What's more, God created them in his own likeness, breathing himself into them—suggesting that, unlike other animals, they share in divine attributes such as language (symbolism), reason, and creativity. He gave them a share in his dominion and made them custodians of his creation. He also told them to replenish the earth: all of humanity descends from them; all of humanity is one big family.

Eden

> *God planted a garden of plenty to the east in Eden, in which he placed man 'to dress it and to keep it'. The garden contained many pleasant and fruitful trees, including, in its centre, the tree of life and the tree of knowledge of good and evil. God said to man, 'Of every tree of the garden thou mayest freely eat: but of the tree of the knowledge of good and evil, thou shalt not eat of it: for in the day that thou eatest thereof thou shalt surely die.'*

In Genesis 2, God creates the Garden of Eden, and man is confirmed as creation's crowning glory. The state of plenty in which man finds himself corresponds to the Golden Age of the Greeks, Hindus, and others: a primordial period of peace and prosperity, innocence and virtue. Many traditions also feature a central tree, vine, pillar, mountain, or other *axis mundi* that bridges Heaven and Earth. For example, in Plato's Myth of Er, souls on the road to rebirth travel to the Spindle of Necessity, a shaft of intensely bright light that extends into the heavens and holds together the universe. The connection to heaven symbolizes man's notion of, and longing for, pure ideals such as love, justice, beauty, and God himself, even though he has never experienced these perfect, or Platonic, forms. In Eden, there are not one but two central trees: the tree of life and the tree of knowledge of good and evil, that is, the tree of moral consciousness, and, by extension, of choice and freedom. God forbids man to eat from the latter tree, warning him that if he does he will die.

Eve

> God said, 'It is not good that the man should be alone...' He
> brought forth every animal for Adam to name, but none proved
> a suitable helpmate. So he brought a deep sleep over Adam, and
> fashioned woman out of one of his ribs. Upon beholding Eve, Adam
> said, 'This is now bone of my bones, and flesh of my flesh: she shall
> be called Woman, because she was taken out of Man.'

Although woman seems to have been created in Genesis 1 ('male
and female created he them'), Genesis 2 finds Adam alone in the
Garden of Eden. This is but one of several inconsistencies, or
apparent inconsistencies, in the genesis story.

God says that 'it is not good that the man should be alone',
suggesting that man is a social animal and unsuited to aloneness.
Adam names the animals, and to name something is to exercise
control over it, and more than that, to exercise language and
symbolic thought, which, as John 1:1 attests, are divine attributes:
'In the beginning was the Word, and the Word was with God, and
the Word was God.' Adam has a share in creation, and a share in
the divine.

Given his superior nature, none of the animals is deemed a suitable
companion for Adam, and God creates Eve from one of Adam's
ribs or sides. Adam himself emphasizes that Eve is as another self,
indicating that man and woman are equal, or, at least, created
equal: 'This is now bone of my bones, and flesh of my flesh...
Therefore shall a man leave his father and his mother, and shall
cleave unto his wife: and they shall be one flesh.' There is a parallel
here with Plato's myth of Aristophanes, according to which human

beings were literally cut into two as a punishment from the gods, and remain incomplete until they are able to find their 'other half'. Both accounts imply marriage and monogamy as the norm for man.

The serpent

> *One day, the serpent, the most subtle of all the beasts in God's creation, took Eve apart and reassured her that she would not die if she ate from the tree of knowledge of good and evil. God lied because 'he doth know that in the day ye eat thereof, then your eyes shall be opened, and ye shall be as gods, knowing good and evil'. Eve took of the fruit and ate, and gave to Adam to eat. 'And the eyes of them both were opened, and they knew that they were naked; and they sewed fig leaves together, and made themselves aprons.'*

Like man, the serpent has the ability to speak and to reason. The only other animal that speaks in the Pentateuch is Balaam's ass, and that's only because God opened its mouth. The serpent is seductive, and phallic in form, and, as I argued in Chapter 1, may represent sexual temptation or adultery, offering up, like the tree itself, the possibilities of choice, freedom, guilt, and remorse.

But of course, it must have been God himself who made the serpent and the tree, and who put them within the reach of man, in the certain knowledge—this being God—that man would eat from the tree. Either man before the fall had no knowledge of good and evil, in which case he was bound to surrender to the serpent; or he did have some knowledge (despite having not yet eaten from the tree), but succumbed to the proud temptation, that is in the nature of man, to rise to the equal of the gods.

Some of the most vivid Greek myths, such as those of Icarus, Oedipus, Sisyphus, and Tantalus, can be read as admonitions against hubris, which is the defiance of the gods from deranged pride, leading to *nemesis*, or downfall. 'Pride goeth before destruction, and an haughty spirit before a fall', and it is also from pride that the angel Lucifer (Lat. 'light-maker') fell from Heaven: 'How art thou fallen from heaven, O Lucifer, son of the morning! … For thou hast said in thine heart, I will ascend into heaven, I will exalt my throne above the stars of God … I will be like the most High.' Although there is no mention in Genesis of Satan or Lucifer, the serpent has often been associated with the devil himself.

The fall

Upon hearing the voice of God, Adam and Eve hid their nakedness among the trees. Adam blamed both Eve and God: 'The woman whom thou gavest to be with me, she gave me of the tree, and I did eat.' Eve in turn blamed the serpent: 'The serpent beguiled me, and I did eat.' God cursed the serpent to go on his belly and eat dust, and put enmity between the serpent and man: '[the seed of man] shall bruise thy head, and thou shalt bruise his heel.' He cursed Eve to the pangs of childbirth, and to marital subservience. He cursed the very ground, condemning Adam to a life of toil and sorrow: 'In the sweat of thy face shalt thou eat bread, till thou return unto the ground, for out of it wast thou taken: for dust thou art, and unto dust shalt thou return.' God clothed Adam and Eve in skins and expelled them from Eden lest Adam, who 'is become as one of us, to know good and evil… put forth his hand, and take also of the tree of life, and eat, and live for ever.' To keep them out of reach of the tree of life, he placed cherubim and a flaming, revolving sword at the gates of Eden.

Pride is one of the seven deadly sins, and it is the sin most hated
by God because it bears all the other sins, and because it blinds
us to truth and reason. For all that, it is arguably the serpent who
spoke the truth, and God who misled, for Adam and Eve did not
die from eating from the tree—or at least not immediately, Adam
being said to have lived 930 years. So either God was jealous of his
own powers, or he set up the tree and the serpent to test man, in
the knowledge that he would succumb.

In later times, Eve took most of the rap for the fall of man. In
his treatise on the apparel of women, the early Christian writer
Tertullian decried women as 'the devil's gateway': 'On account of
your desert,' he vituperated, 'even the Son of God had to die.' Eve
serves as a warning to man, and especially woman, that to disobey
is to court disaster. But the misogyny in Genesis is by no means
a cultural exception. Eve's counterpart in Greek myth is the first
woman Pandora, who was sent to man in punishment for sharing
in the fire that Prometheus had stolen from the other gods: by
neglecting the warning not to open the jar of evils, she brought
the Golden Age of Man to a close. Greek myth is littered with
dangerous and destructive temptresses such as Circe, Medea, and
the sirens, and even fair Helen is chiefly remembered for sparking
the Trojan War.

But just as Prometheus delivered stolen fire to man, so Eve, and
the serpent, delivered man into self-consciousness, setting him
up, were it not for his short lifespan, as rival to God. At the same
time, man's self-consciousness removed him from nature into a
life of toil, doubt, fear, guilt, shame, blame, enmity, loneliness, and
frailty—and the product of this separation, the fruit and flower of
this exile, is, of course, culture.

'God,' said the writer Victor Hugo (1802–1885), 'made only water, but man made wine.'

12

Sex, sexuality, and duplicity in Ancient Rome

In Ancient Rome, infant daughters were more likely to be exposed (abandoned) than infant sons because they would not carry the family name and would require a dowry to wed. Although girls from leading families were taught to read and write, the vast majority did not receive any formal education. A woman married soon after puberty, and her highest duty, both to her husband and to Rome, was to bear a vigorous son who might one day follow in his father's name and estate. A woman could marry *cum manu*, becoming, in legal terms, a daughter of her husband; or *sine manu* in which case she could hold property in her name. But a woman who had married *sine manu* had to have a guardian or tutor, usually her father, who would determine how she could or couldn't use her property. A tutor had considerable powers, and could force his tutee out of one marriage and into another, more expedient one. That said, not all families observed these practices, particularly if the head of the family had died on campaign; and by the time of Augustus (R 27 BC–14 AD), citizen women with at least three children became legally independent or *sui iuris*.

Roman women, even if *sui iuris*, could not vote or assume public
office, and upper class women in particular were largely confined
to running the home. But in contrast to the women of Classical
Athens, who were regarded as chattel and were, in some respects,
worse off than slaves, Roman women played an important
role in the raising of children, including their male children;
and, although they were forbidden to drink of the adulterous
wine, or to be seen on stage, they were otherwise free to attend
dinner parties, baths, and circuses. There were, of course, a
few formidable women who broke with convention, and many
if not most women exercised an important influence over their
husbands, sons, and brothers—even when, as with Agrippina the
Younger (15–59 AD), these happened to be emperors. According
to Tacitus, Agrippina visited astrologers to ask about the future of
her son, Nero. The astrologers predicted that Nero would become
emperor, and would kill her. Agrippina replied, "Let him kill me,
so long as he becomes emperor."

Both women and men, but especially women, were supposed
to uphold *pudicitia*, a complex virtue that can be translated as
restraint or chastity. A woman with a high degree of *pudicitia*, that
is, a *univira* or 'one-man woman', sought at all times to appear
modest and to limit her social interactions with men other than
her husband and male relatives. However, divorce did not attract
any stigma or prejudice, and upper class divorcees or widows were
encouraged, even expected, to remarry after a suitable period
of mourning. *Pudicitia* stood for reason and control, whereas
impudicitia—that is, shamelessness and sexual vice (*stuprum*,
'sex crime')—stood for chaos and disaster. A *univira* was held in
high esteem and even idealized, with Augustus going so far as
to enact a programme of legislation to promote the notion and

its observance—and, at the same time, sending his promiscuous daughter and only biological child Julia into permanent exile. According to Suetonius, Augustus quoted Hector in Homer's *Iliad*: 'Ah, never to have married, and childless to have died!' The historian Livy (59 BC–17 AD) upheld the legendary figure of Lucretia as the epitome of *pudicitia*, and it is possible that her rape and subsequent suicide are an allegorical tale constructed to uphold Roman values and justify the rise of the Republic from the dunghill of the monarchy.

All this is not to say that the Romans were prudes, or that they never lost sight of their high ideals. Later Christians may have exaggerated the degree of their depravity, but it cannot be denied that they had, to say the least, ambivalent attitudes towards sex. In contrast to their women, it was entirely accepted and even expected for freeborn men to have extramarital relations with both female and male partners, especially adolescents, provided that they (1) exercised moderation, (2) adopted the active, or dominating, role, and (3) confined their activities to slaves and prostitutes, or, less commonly, a concubine or 'kept woman'. Married or marriageable women who belonged to another freeborn man were strictly off limits, as were young male citizens. The first century Stoic philosopher Musonius, a rare voice at the time, criticized the double standard that granted men much greater sexual freedom than women, arguing that, if men are to presume to exercise control over women, they ought to exercise even greater control over themselves.

The Romans sought to control female sexuality to protect the family and, by extension, social order, prosperity, and the state. They crystallized these notions in the cult of Venus, the mother

of Aeneas, founder of Rome; and in the priestesses of the hearth
goddess Vesta, the Vestal Virgins, who ran the risk of being buried
alive if convicted of fornication. To violate a Vestal Virgin's vow
of chastity was to commit an act of religious impurity (*incestum*),
and thereby to undermine Rome's compact with the gods, the
pax deorum ('peace of the gods'). Roman religion very much
reflected and regulated sexual mores, with the male-female duality
enshrined in the pairings of the 12 *Dii Consentes* or major deities
(the Roman equivalent of the Greek Olympian gods): Jupiter-Juno,
Neptune-Minerva, Mars-Venus, Apollo-Diana, Vulcan-Vesta, and
Mercury-Ceres. Many religious festivals, such as the Liberalia,
Floralia, and Lupercalia, to say nothing of the banned Bacchanalia,
incorporated an important element of sexuality, as discussed in
Chapter 7.

The Vestal Virgins tended, among others duties, to the cult of the
fascinus populi Romani, the sacred image of the divine phallus and
male counterpart of the hearth of Vesta. Like the Palladium, Lares,
and Penates of Troy and the eternal fire, the *fascinus populi Romani*
assured the ascendency and continuity of the state. Similarly,
during the Liberalia, devotees of Liber Pater carted a giant phallus
through the countryside to fertilize the land and safeguard the
crops—after which a virtuous matron placed a wreath on top of the
phallus. Smaller talismans in the form of a penis and testes, often
winged, invoked the protection of the god Fascinus against the evil
eye. These charms, or *fascini*, often in the form of a ring or amulet,
were most commonly worn by infants, boys, and soldiers.

A freeborn man's *libertas* or political liberty manifested itself,
among others, in the mastery of his own body; and his adoption
of a passive or submissive sexual position implied servility and a

loss of virility. Homosexual behaviour among soldiers not only violated the decorum against intercourse among freeborn men, but also compromised the penetrated soldier's sexual and therefore military dominance, with rape and penetration the symbols— and sometimes also the realities—of military defeat. According to the historian Polybius, who wrote in the 2nd century BC, the penalty for a soldier who had allowed himself to be penetrated was *fustuarium*, that is, cudgelling to death, the same punishment as for desertion.

Latin does not have a strict equivalent for the noun 'homosexual', which is relatively recent in coinage and concept; but a minority of men did, then as now, express a clear same-sex preference or orientation—most famously the emperor Hadrian (R 117–138 AD), who founded a city in memory of his beloved Antinous and even had him deified. Nero actually married his freedman Pythagoras in a public ceremony in which he took the role of the bride. Later in his reign, he favoured a young boy called Sporus, whom he castrated and married. This time Nero took on the role of the groom, and had Sporus appear in public in the regalia of a Roman empress. In one of his many footnotes, the 18th century historian Edward Gibbon conceded that 'of the first fifteen emperors, Claudius was the only one whose taste in love was entirely correct'—by which he meant 'heterosexual'.

Most extramarital and same-sex activity took place with slaves and prostitutes. Slaves were regarded as property, and lacked the legal standing that protected a citizen's body. A freeman who forced a slave into having sex could not be charged with rape, but only under laws relating to property damage, and then only at the instigation of the slave's owner. Prostitution was both legal and common, and often operated out of brothels or the fornices (arcade dens) under the arches of a circus. Most prostitutes were slaves or freedwomen. By becoming a prostitute, a freeborn person suffered *infamia*, that is, loss of respect or reputation, and became an *infamis*, losing her or his social and legal standing. Other groups that incurred *infamia*—a concept that still retains some currency in the Roman Catholic Church—included actors, dancers, gladiators, and other entertainers. Members of these groups, which had in common the pleasuring of others, that is, objectification, could be subjected to violence and even killed with relative impunity. By some twisted Roman logic, a man who was anally penetrated was seen to take on the role of a woman, but a woman who was anally penetrated was seen to take on the role of a boy. In a poem that had long been censored, Martial's wife catches him with a boy. When she offers him anal intercourse to encourage fidelity, he replies mockingly that anal sex with boys cannot compare to anal sex with women: 'you, my wife, have got no more than two cunts.'

Since Roman men could and often did indulge in extramarital sex, it might be assumed that Roman marriage was all duty and dour. However, the bedrooms of the nobility were often decorated with erotic scenes ranging from elegant dalliance to explicit pornography. Horace had a mirrored room for sex, and Tiberius (R 14–37 AD) stocked his bedrooms with the sex manuals of one Elephantis. In Ancient Rome as in Victorian England, virtuous restraint often went hand in hand with licentious abandon, the one exposed to the glare of the public arena and the other hidden away in closed rooms and shady nooks.

And so, according to Seneca:

Virtue you will find in the temple, in the forum, in the senate house, standing before the city walls, dusty and sunburnt, her hands rough; pleasure you will most often find lurking around the baths and sweating rooms, and places that fear the police, in search of darkness, soft, effete, reeking of wine and perfume, pallid or else painted and made up with cosmetics like a corpse.

13

How love became the new religion

So I'm thanking you today because of you I am now me.

—John Butler Trio, *Fool for You*

In the fifth century BC, the Greek philosopher Empedocles held that there are four primordial elements: air, earth, fire, and water. These elements are driven together and apart by the opposed cosmic principles of Love and Strife. Love brings the elements together, and unopposed Love leads to 'The One', a divine and resplendent sphere. Strife gradually degrades the sphere, returning it to the elements, and this cosmic cycle repeats itself *ad infinitum*. According to legend, Empedocles killed himself by leaping into the flames of Mount Etna, either to prove that he was immortal or to make people believe that he was. In his poem *Empedocles on Etna* (1852), Matthew Arnold put the following last words into his mouth:

> *The heart will glow no more; thou art*
> *A living man no more, Empedocles!*
> *Nothing but a devouring flame of thought—*

But a naked, eternally restless mind!
To the elements it came from
Everything will return
Our bodies to earth,
Our blood to water,
Heat to fire,
Breath to air.
They were well born, they will be well entomb'd—
But mind?

Empedocles may have conceived of love as a great cosmic principle, but it is in fact Plato who transformed it into the spiritual, transcendental, and redemptory force that it has become. Before Plato, and for a long time after, some people did, of course, fall in love, but they did not believe that their love might in some sense save them. When, in Homer's *Iliad*, Helen eloped with Paris, neither she nor he thought of their attraction as pure or noble or elevating. The Greeks recognized several types of love (Chapter 17): the one that most approaches our modern concept of romantic love is *eros*, or passionate love. Rather than celebrating *eros*, Greek myth sees it as a kind of madness induced by one of Cupid's arrows. The arrow breaches us and we 'fall' in love, often with disastrous consequences such as, well, the Trojan War. In the *Antigone* of Sophocles, the chorus sings: 'Love… whoever feels your grip is driven mad… you wrench the minds of the righteous into outrage, swerve them to their ruin…' In Homer's *Odyssey*, despite her many suitors, Penelope remains faithful to her husband Odysseus. But her commitment is better understood in terms of dutiful love, or connubial fidelity, than modern, madcap romantic love. When Odysseus finally returns and slaughters all the suitors, Penelope is reluctant even to recognize him.

Plato's *Symposium* (4th century BC) contains a myth about the origins of human love, the so-called myth of Aristophanes. Once upon a time, there were three kinds of people: male, descended from the sun; female, descended from the earth; and hermaphrodite, with both male and female parts, descended from the moon. These early people were completely round, each with four arms and four legs, two identical faces on opposite sides of a head with four ears, and all else to match. They walked both forwards and backwards, and ran by turning cartwheels on their eight limbs, moving in circles like their parents the planets. They were powerful and unruly, and sought to scale the heavens. So Zeus, the father of the gods, cut them into two 'like a sorb-apple which is halved for pickling', and even threatened to cut them into two again, so that they might hop about on one leg. After that, people searched all over for their missing part. When they finally found it, they wrapped themselves around it very tightly and did not let go. This is the origin of our desire for others: those of us who desire members of the opposite sex used to be hermaphrodites, whereas men who desire men used to be male, and women who desire women used to be female. When we find our *other half* (the expression descends from Plato's myth), we are 'lost in an amazement of love and friendship and intimacy' that cannot be accounted for by a simple drive for sex, but by a desire to be whole again and restored to our original nature.

Later in Plato's *Symposium*, Socrates relates a conversation that he once had with the priestess Diotima, from whom he supposedly learnt the art of love. According to Diotima, a youth should be taught to love one beautiful body so that he comes to realize that this beautiful body shares beauty with other beautiful bodies, and thus that it is foolish to love just one beautiful body. In loving all beautiful bodies, the youth comes to understand that the beauty of the soul is superior to that of the body, and begins to love those who are beautiful in soul regardless of whether they are also beautiful in body. Once he has transcended the physical, he discovers that beautiful practices and customs and the various kinds of knowledge also share in a common beauty. Finally, arriving at the summit of the ladder of love, he is able to experience Beauty itself, rather than its various apparitions. By exchanging the various apparitions of virtue for Virtue itself, he gains immortality and the love of the gods.

Although Plato's model eventually gained the upper hand, other models of love in antiquity are the perfect friendship of Plato's one-time student Aristotle, and the naturalism of the Roman poets Lucretius and Ovid. For Aristotle, friendships founded on advantage alone, or pleasure alone, are as nothing compared to those founded on virtue. To be in such a friendship, and to seek out the good of one's friend, is to exercise reason and virtue, which is the distinctive function of human beings, and which amounts to happiness. In a virtuous friendship, our friend is as another self, and to seek out his good is also to seek out our own. Unfortunately, the number of people with whom one can sustain a perfect friendship is very small, first, because reason and virtue are not to be found in everyone (never, for instance, in young people, who are not wise enough to be virtuous), and, second, because perfect friendship can only be formed and sustained if the pair of friends spend a great deal of exclusive time investing into each other.

> *Perfect friendship is the friendship of men who are good, and alike in virtue; for these wish well alike to each other qua good, and they*

are good themselves. Now those who wish well to their friends for their sake are most truly friends; for they do this by reason of their own nature and not incidentally; therefore their friendship lasts as long as they are good—and goodness is an enduring thing.

A paradigm of perfect friendship, albeit from a very different time and place, is that between the essayist Michel de Montaigne (1533–1592) and the humanist Etienne de la Boétie (1530–1563). The two men became the closest friends from the moment they met at a feast in Bordeaux. Montaigne wrote that friendship, 'having seized my whole will, led it to plunge and lose itself in his.' 'Our souls mingle and blend with each other so completely that they efface the seam that joined them, and cannot find it again.' He struggled to explain this enthrallment: 'If you press me to say why I loved him, I can say no more than it was because he was he, and I was I.' The young men had much in common, including their privileged backgrounds, soaring intellects, and refined sensibilities. But more importantly, they shared a devotion to classical and Aristotelian ideals of the good life, which had prepared the ground in which their friendship could blossom into one so fine that 'it is a lot if fortune can do it once in three centuries'. In a sonnet, la Boétie declaimed: 'You have been bound to me, Montaigne, both by the power of nature and by virtue, which is the sweet allurement of love.' The married Montaigne never fully recovered from la Boétie's premature death from the plague, and for the rest of his life felt like 'no more than a half person'. No one, he warned, should ever be 'joined and glued to us so strongly that they cannot be detached without tearing off our skin and some part of our flesh as well.' Compared to the four years of friendship with la Boétie, the rest of his life seemed 'but smoke and ashes, a night dark and dreary'. It is sobering to think that, had the Aristotelian template not been available to them, their friendship may never have flown. Love, like madness, can only fill the models that society makes available.

Lucretius (99–55 BC) and Ovid (43 BC–17/18 AD) did not idealize love, seeing it neither as a track to transcendence, like Plato, nor a vehicle of virtue, like Aristotle. Instead, they thought of it merely as thinly garbed animal instinct, a kind of insanity that could nonetheless be enjoyed if tamed by reason and sublimed into art. 'Love,' said Ovid, 'is a thing ever filled with anxious fear.' *Pauperibus vates ego sum, quia pauper amavi*: 'I am the poet of the poor, for I was poor when I loved.' The modern heirs to Lucretius and Ovid are Schopenhauer, and, later, Freud and Proust. In his masterpiece, *The World as Will* (1819), Schopenhauer argues that beneath the world of appearances lies the world of will, a fundamentally blind process of striving and reproduction. Everything in the world is a manifestation of will, including the human body: the genitals are objectified sexual impulse, the mouth and digestive tract objectified hunger, and so on. Even our higher faculties have evolved for no other purpose than to help us meet the demands of will. The most powerful manifestation of will is the impulse for sex. The will-to-life of the yet unconceived offspring draws man and woman together in a shared delusion of lust and love. But with the task accomplished, the delusion fades away and they return to their 'original narrowness and neediness'.

On the eastern edge of the Mediterranean, the Jewish and Christian models of love developed alongside the classical models. In Genesis 22, God asks Abraham to sacrifice his beloved son Isaac. But as Abraham is about to slay Isaac, an angel stays his hand: 'now I know that thou fearest God, seeing thou hast not withheld thy son, thine only son, from me.' It is true that the Old Testament instructs us to love God (Deuteronomy 6:4–5) and to love our neighbours (Leviticus 19:18). However, the Binding of Isaac underlines that, although love and morality are important principles, unquestioning obedience or allegiance to God is more important still, for God is morality, and God is love. In contrast, the New Testament elevates love into the supreme virtue and commingles it with life and death. More than a commandment, love becomes the royal road to redemption: 'He that loveth not his brother abideth in death. Whosoever hateth his brother is a murderer: and ye know that no murderer hath eternal life abiding in him.' One must even turn the other cheek to love one's enemies: 'Love your enemies, bless them that curse you, do good to them that hate you, and pray for them which despitefully use you, and persecute you.' Jesus may have spoken Greek, and might have come under the direct or indirect influence of Platonism. Whether or not he did, over the centuries, the Church doctors sought to align Christian theology with classical philosophy, especially Platonism; and Christian love, more properly called charity, and ultimately aimed at God, blurred with something much more self-oriented.

The blending of Christian love and Platonism laid the ground for the troubadour tradition that began in late 11th century Occitania (broadly, the southern half of France). A troubadour extolled refined or courtly love, which he directed at a married and unavailable lady, often of a superior social rank, as a means of exalting himself and attaining to a higher virtue, notably by carrying out a succession of chivalrous acts or tests. For the first time in the Judeo-Christian tradition, love, insofar as courtly love can be counted as love, did not ultimately aim at, or depend upon, God, and the Church duly declared it a heresy. In a significant cultural reversal, the daughter of Eve, although in this context an essentially passive and interchangeable idol, turned from devilish temptress to sublime conduit of virtue, a goddess in the place of God. The troubadour tradition remained an elite and minority movement, and died out around the time of the Black Death in 1348.

Saint Francis of Assisi (d. 1226) taught that nature is the mirror of God. Although a reforming Christian, his *Canticle of the Creatures* comes across as almost pagan in inspiration: 'Be praised, my Lord, through all your creatures, especially through my lord Brother Sun, who brings the day; and you give light through him. And he is beautiful and radiant in all his splendour! Of you, Most High, he bears the likeness.' In the next period, God gradually comes down to earth, to be worshipped through his creation, and, above all, through the human body. This, in any case, served as justification for all those Renaissance nudes, first among them Michelangelo's magisterial statue of David (1504) which the Florentines displayed at the historical and political heart of their city in the Piazza della Signoria. One could admire David, or anyone else for that matter, as the mirror of God, but, for just that reason, one could not turn him into an object of lust. God's earthly descent ends, and he hits the ground, with the Dutch philosopher Baruch de Spinoza (1632–1677), who thought of God and nature as one and the same. More precisely, Spinoza brought nature into God, thereby, in some sense, eliminating or radically redefining him: 'Whatsoever is, is in God... God is the indwelling, and not the transient cause of all things.'

As God retreated from love, Platonism, which had always been lurking in the background, stepped forward to fill the void. Abraham had surrendered himself and his son Isaac out of devotion to God. But in the Romantic era, love became all the opposite: a means of finding and validating oneself. 'So I'm thanking you today because of you I am now me.' In the time of God, finding oneself—or, more accurately, losing oneself to God—had required years of patient spiritual practice, but, after the French Revolution, romantic love could save almost anyone, and with very little investment on their part. Plato's ladder of love had been an elitist project designed to sublime sexual desire into virtue, but the Romantics, concerned with neither God nor reason, held that love with a good and beautiful person could only intensify sexual desire. The sacred seeped out of God and into love, and, with more success than reason, progress, communism, or any other -ism, love took the place of the dying religion in lending weight and meaning and texture to our lives. People had once loved God, but now they loved love: more than with their beloved, they, like the troubadours before them, fell in love with love itself.

14

The psychology of romantic love

In the last chapter, we looked at how love became the new religion. In this chapter, we look at some of the psychology underlying that position.

The eponymous hero—or antihero—of *Don Quixote* by Miguel de Cervantes (1547–1616) idealizes his 'princess' to such an extent that it becomes comical. To emulate the knights-errant of old who fought battles to earn the affections of their true love, Don Quixote identifies a simple peasant girl called Aldonza Lorenzo, changes her name to the much more romantic and aristocratic sounding 'Dulcinea del Toboso', and paints her in the most flattering terms possible—even though he has only ever seen her fleetingly and never spoken to her. Dulcinea barely exists outside his imagination, but the idea of her nonetheless keeps Don Quixote alive on his quest:

> ...her name is Dulcinea, her country El Toboso, a village of La Mancha, her rank must be at least that of a princess, since she is my queen and lady, and her beauty superhuman, since all the impossible and fanciful attributes of beauty which the poets apply to their ladies are verified in her; for her hairs are gold, her forehead

Elysian fields, her eyebrows rainbows, her eyes suns, her cheeks roses, her lips coral, her teeth pearls, her neck alabaster, her bosom marble, her hands ivory, her fairness snow, and what modesty conceals from sight such, I think and imagine, as rational reflection can only extol, not compare.

The ego defence of idealization involves overestimating the positive attributes of a person, object, or idea, while underestimating or overlooking the negative ones: but more fundamentally, it involves the projection of our needs and desires onto that person, object, or idea. The classic example of idealization is that of being infatuated, when love is confused with a need to love, and the idealized person's negative attributes are not only minimized but turned into positive attributes and thought of as endearing. Although this can make for a rude awakening, there are few better ways of relieving our existential anxiety than by manufacturing something that is 'perfect' for us, be it a piece of equipment, a place, country, person, or god.

But even a god is not enough. According to St Augustine, man is prone to a curious feeling of dissatisfaction accompanied by a subtle sense of longing for something undefined. This uneasy state arises from his fallen condition: although he has an innate potential to relate to God or the absolute, this potential can never be fully realized, and so he yearns for other things to fill its place. Yet these other things do not satisfy, and he is left with an insatiable feeling of longing—longing for something that cannot be defined.

In *Surprised by Joy* (1955), the writer CS Lewis calls this feeling of longing 'joy', which he describes as 'an unsatisfied desire which is itself more desirable than any other satisfaction', and which I sometimes think of—in the broadest sense—as a sort of aesthetic and creative reservoir. The paradox of 'joy' arises from the self-defeating nature of human desire, which might be thought of as nothing other than a desire for desire, a longing for longing.

In the *Weight of Glory*, Lewis illustrates this from the age-old quest for beauty:

The books or the music in which we thought the beauty was located will betray us if we trust to them; it was not in them, it only came through them, and what came through them was longing. These things—the beauty, the memory of our own past—are good images of what we really desire; but if they are mistaken for the thing itself they turn into dumb idols, breaking the hearts of their worshippers. For they are not the thing itself; they are only the scent of a flower we have not found, the echo of a tune we have not heard, news from a country we have not visited.

This chapter is adapted from the chapter on idealization in *Hide and Seek: The Psychology of Self-Deception.*

15

The history of kissing

In some respects, the history of kissing parallels the history of romantic love. Kissing is not universal among human beings. Even today, there are some cultures from which it remains completely absent. This suggests that, like romantic love, it is neither innate nor intuitive.

One possibility is that it is a learned behaviour that evolved from 'kiss feeding', the process by which mothers in some cultures feed their babies by passing masticated food from mouth to mouth. However, there are some contemporary indigenous cultures that still practise kiss feeding, but not social or erotic kissing. Another possibility is that it is a culturally-determined form of grooming behaviour; and, at least in the case of erotic or deep kissing, a representation, substitute for, and complement to, penetrative intercourse.

Whatever the case, kissing behaviour is not unique to human beings: primates such as Bonobo apes frequently kiss one another, and dogs and cats lick and nuzzle one another, as well as members of other species; even snails and insects partake in antennal play. It could be that, rather than kissing, these animals are in fact grooming, smelling, or communicating with one another, but, even so, their behaviour implies and furthers trust and bonding.

Vedic texts from Ancient India seem to refer to kissing, and the *Kama Sutra* (2nd century AD) devotes an entire chapter to modes of kissing. Some anthropologists have suggested that the Greeks learnt about erotic kissing from the Indians when Alexander the Great crossed into India in 326 BC, but, even if true, it need not imply that erotic kissing originated in India.

In Homer's *Iliad*, which dates back to the 9th century BC, King Priam memorably kisses Achilles' hand to plead for the return of his son's cadaver:

> *Fear, O Achilles, the wrath of heaven; think of your own father and have compassion upon me, who am the more pitiable, for I have steeled myself as no man yet has ever steeled himself before me, and have raised to my lips the hand of him who slew my son.*

In the *Histories* (5th century BC), Herodotus speaks of kissing among the Persians, who greeted men of equal rank with a kiss on the mouth and those of slightly lower rank with a kiss on the cheek. He also reports that, because Greeks ate of the cow, which was sacred in Egypt, the Egyptians would not kiss them on the mouth.

Kisses also feature in the Old Testament. Disguised as Esau, Jacob kisses the blind Isaac, thereby stealing his brother's blessing. In the Song of Songs, which seems to celebrate sexual love, one of the lovers implores, 'Let him kiss me with the kisses of his mouth, for thy love is better than wine.'

Under the Romans, kissing became much more widespread. The Romans kissed their partners or lovers, family and friends, and rulers. They distinguished a kiss on the hand or cheek (*osculum*) from a kiss on the lips (*basium*) and a deep or passionate kiss (*savolium*). Roman poets such as Ovid and Catullus celebrated kissing, as, for example, in *Catullus 8*:

> *Goodbye girl, now Catullus is firm,*
> *he doesn't search for you, won't ask unwillingly.*
> *But you'll grieve, when nobody asks.*
> *Woe to you, wicked girl, what life's left for you?*
> *Who'll submit to you now? Who'll see your beauty?*
> *Who now will you love? Whose will they say you'll be?*
> *Who will you kiss? Whose lips will you bite?*
> *But you, Catullus, be resolved to be firm.*

Roman kisses served many purposes from the social and political to the erotic and sexual. The social status of a Roman citizen determined the part of the body on which he could kiss the emperor, from cheek down to foot. In an age of illiteracy, kisses served to seal agreements—whence the expression 'to seal with a kiss' and the 'x' on the dotted line. Couples got married by kissing in front of a gathered assembly, a custom that has been carried into modern times (Chapter 26).

Practices changed with the decline of Rome and the rise of Christianity. Early Christians often greeted one another with a 'holy kiss', which they believed led to a transfer of spirit. The Latin *anima* means both 'breath of air' and 'soul', and like *animus* ('mind'), derives from the Proto-Indo-European root *ane-* ('to breathe or blow'). Although St Peter had spoken of the 'kiss of charity', and St Paul of the 'holy kiss', early Church sects omitted kissing on Maundy Thursday, which marks the date on which Judas betrayed Jesus with a kiss: 'But Jesus said unto him, Judas, betrayest thou the Son of man with a kiss?' Outside the Church, kissing was used to cement rank and maintain social order, with, for example, subjects and vassals kissing the robe of the king, or the ring or slippers of the pope.

After the fall of Rome, the lovers' kiss seems to have disappeared for several centuries, only to re-emerge at the end of the 11th century with courtly love. The kiss of Romeo and Juliet is emblematic of this wider movement, which sought to remove courtship from the purview of family and society, and to celebrate love no longer as a dutiful act but as a liberating and potentially subversive force. Yet, the fate of the star-crossed lovers reminds us that such careless abandon is not without risks, and it could be that the concept of vampirism evolved as a representation of the dangers—to health, rank, reputation, prospects, and happiness—of kissing the wrong person.

This chapter is adapted from the chapter on kissing in *Heaven and Hell: The Psychology of the Emotions*.

16

Who was Valentine?

St Valentine is an icon of romantic love, and his feast day is growing in cultural and commercial importance. But who was Valentine?

In 496, Pope Gelasius I established St Valentine's February 14th feast day, perhaps to Christianize the loud and irreverent Lupercalia. Celebrated on the ides of February, the Lupercalia had come to replace the spring cleansing ritual of Februa, which gave the month its name. By purifying the city and purging it of evil spirits, the festivities brought health, vigour, and fertility. Priests sacrificed a goat and a dog before the image of Lupercus in the Lupercal, the cave in which the she-wolf (*lupa*) had suckled Romulus and Remus, the descendants of Aeneas and mythical founders of Rome.

The origins of St Valentine (or *Valentinus*, 'strength') are so obscure that, in 1969, the Catholic Church removed him from the General Roman (liturgical) Calendar. There are at least three early Christian saints by the name of Valentinus. One was a priest in Rome, the second was a bishop in Terni, and the third was martyred in Africa. Whichever one he was, the St Valentine commemorated in the feast day rose to become the Patron Saint of courtly love, lovers, affianced couples, and happy marriages, and also beekeepers, epilepsy, fainting, and plague, among others.

Over time, legends grew around the St Valentine of the feast day. According to one prominent legend, he was a priest who fell foul of the emperor Claudius II. In the belief that bachelors make better soldiers, Claudius prohibited marriage for young men, but Valentine continued to marry them, and, when challenged, attempted to convert Claudius to Christianity. To punish him for his insolence, Claudius ordered that he be beaten, stoned, and beheaded. While in prison awaiting his calvary, Valentine fell in love, or made friends, with Julia, the blind daughter of his gaoler Asterius, and sent her secret letters signed 'from your Valentine'. When Valentine miraculously restored Julia's sight, Asterius converted to Christianity.

It is not until the era of courtly love in the Middle Ages that the feast of St Valentine became linked with romantic love. The earliest evidence of this association is from *Parlement of Foules* (1382), a poem by Chaucer to honour the first anniversary of the engagement of Richard II and Anne of Bohemia: 'For this was on St Valentine's Day (*seynt Volantynys day*)/ When every bird/bride (*byrd*) cometh there to choose his mate.' The earliest evidence of a person actually being a valentine is from a rondeau (a mediaeval verse form) to his wife from Charles, Duke of Orléans, who had been captured at the Battle of Agincourt (1415) and locked up in the Tower of London: *Je suis desja d'amour tanné/ Ma tres douce Valentinée…*

Valentine's Day as a romantic holiday was popularized by Shakespeare, with these lines in *Hamlet* (~1602) spoken by Ophelia: 'To-morrow is Saint Valentine's day/ All in the morning betime/ And I a maid at your window/ To be your Valentine.' By the 18th century, the giving of gifts and the exchanging of cards made of lace and ribbon had become commonplace in England. In the 19th century, the custom spread throughout the English-speaking world, and, in the late 20th century, well beyond. Today, Americans spend over 18 billion dollars a year celebrating Valentine's Day, which, after Christmas, has become the most popular card-sending holiday. Women buy 85 per cent of all Valentine's Day cards, but men buy over 70 per cent of the flowers and, according to the National Retail Federation, fork out twice as much overall. As for poor Valentine, we may never know who he was, but what we do know is that he loved God more than any mortal.

17

The 7 types of love

Everyone seems to be hankering after romantic love, but few of us realize that, far from being timeless and universal, romantic love is in fact a modern construct, one that emerged in tandem with the novel. In *Madame Bovary* (1856), itself a novel, Gustave Flaubert tells us that Emma Bovary only found out about romantic love through 'the refuse of old lending libraries'. These books, he wrote:

> …*were all about love and lovers, damsels in distress swooning in lonely lodges, postillions slaughtered all along the road, horses ridden to death on every page, gloomy forests, troubles of the heart, vows, sobs, tears, kisses, rowing-boats in the moonlight, nightingales in the grove, gentlemen brave as lions and gentle as lambs, too virtuous to be true, invariably well-dressed, and weeping like fountains.*

But there are many other ways to love, not all of which are consistent or consonant with romantic love. By preoccupying ourselves with romantic love, we risk neglecting other types of love that are more readily accessible and that may, especially in the longer term, prove more healing and fulfilling.

The seven types of love discussed below are loosely based on classical readings, especially of Plato and Aristotle, and on J.A. Lee's 1973 book *Colours of Love*.

1. *Eros* is sexual or passionate love, and is the type most akin to our modern construct of romantic love. In Greek myth, it is a form of madness brought about by one of Cupid's arrows. The arrow breaches us and we 'fall' in love, as did Paris with Helen, leading to the Trojan War and the downfall of Troy and much of the assembled Greek army. In modern times, *eros* has been amalgamated with the broader life force, something akin to Schopenhauer's will, a fundamentally blind process of striving for survival and reproduction. Eros has also been contrasted with *logos*, or reason, and Cupid painted as a blindfolded child.

2. The hallmark of *philia*, or friendship, is shared goodwill. Aristotle believed that a person can bear goodwill to another for one of three reasons: that he is useful; that he is pleasant; and, above all, that he is good, that is, rational and virtuous. Friendships founded on goodness are associated not only with mutual benefit but also with companionship, dependability, and trust.

For Plato, the best kind of friendship is that which lovers have for each other. It is a *philia* born out of *eros*, and that in turn feeds back into *eros* to strengthen and develop it, transforming it from a lust for possession into a shared desire for a higher level of understanding of the self, the other, and the world. In short, *philia* transforms *eros* from a lust for possession into an impulse for philosophy. Real friends seek together to live truer, fuller lives by relating to each other authentically and teaching each other about the limitations of their beliefs and the defects in their character, which are a far greater source of error than mere rational confusion: they are, in effect, each other's therapist—and in that much it helps to find a friend with some degree of openness, articulacy, and insight, both to change and to be changed.

3. *Storge* ('store-gae'), or familial love, is a kind of *philia* pertaining to the love between parents and their children. It differs from most *philia* in that it tends, especially with younger children, to be unilateral or asymmetrical. More broadly, *storge* is the fondness born out of familiarity or dependency and, unlike *eros* or *philia*, does not hang on our personal qualities. People in the early stages of a romantic relationship often expect unconditional *storge*, but find only the need and dependency of *eros*, and, if they are lucky, the maturity and fertility of *philia*. Given enough time, *eros* tends to mutate into *storge*.

4. *Agape* is universal love, such as the love for strangers, nature, or God. Unlike *storge*, it does not depend on filiation or familiarity. Also called charity by Christian thinkers, *agape* can be said to encompass the modern concept of altruism, defined as unselfish concern for the welfare of others. Recent studies link altruism with a number of benefits. In the short term, altruism leaves us with a euphoric feeling—the so-called 'helper's high'. In the longer term, it is associated with better mental and physical health, as well as longevity. At a social level, altruism serves as a signal of cooperative intentions, and also of resource availability and so of mating or partnering potential. It also opens up a debt account, encouraging beneficiaries to reciprocate with gifts and favours that may be of much greater value to us than those with which we feel ready to part. More generally, altruism, or *agape*, helps to build and maintain the psychological, social, and, indeed, environmental

fabric that shields, sustains, and enriches us. Given the increasing anger and division in our society, and the state of our planet, we could all do with quite a bit more *agape*.

5. *Ludus* is playful or uncommitted love. It can involve activities such as teasing and dancing, or more overt flirting, seducing, and conjugating. The focus is on fun, and sometimes also on conquest, with no strings attached. *Ludus* relationships are casual, undemanding, and uncomplicated but, for all that, can be very long-lasting. *Ludus* works best when both parties are mature and self-sufficient. Problems arise when one party mistakes *ludus* for *eros*, whereas *ludus* is in fact much more compatible with *philia*.

6. *Pragma* is a kind of practical love founded on reason or duty and one's longer-term interests. Sexual attraction takes a back seat in favour of personal qualities and compatibilities, shared goals, and making it work. In the days of arranged marriages, *pragma* must have been very common. Although unfashionable, it remains widespread, most visibly in certain high-profile celebrity and political pairings. Many relationships that begin with *eros* or *ludus* end up in various combinations of *storge* and *pragma*. *Pragma* may seem opposed to *ludus*, but the two can co-exist, with the one providing a counterpoint to the other. In the best of cases, the partners in the *pragma* relationship agree to turn a blind eye—or even a sympathetic eye, as in the case of Simone de Beauvoir and Jean-Paul Sartre, or Vita Sackville-West and Harold Nicholson.

7. *Philautia* is self-love, which can be healthy or unhealthy. Unhealthy self-love is akin to hubris. In Ancient Greece, a person could be accused of hubris if he placed himself above the gods, or, like certain modern politicians, above the greater good. Many

believed that hubris led to destruction, or *nemesis*. Today, hubris has come to mean an inflated sense of one's status, abilities, or accomplishments, especially when accompanied by haughtiness or arrogance. As it disregards truth, hubris promotes injustice, conflict, and enmity.

Healthy self-love is akin to self-esteem, which is our cognitive and, above all, emotional appraisal of our own worth relative to that of others. More than that, it is the matrix through which we think, feel, and act, and reflects and determines our relation to ourselves, to others, and to the world.

Self-esteem and self-confidence do not always go hand in hand. In particular, it is possible to be highly self-confident and yet to have profoundly low self-esteem, as is the case with many performers and celebrities.

People with high self-esteem do not need to prop themselves up with externals such as income, status, or notoriety, or lean on crutches such as alcohol, drugs, or sex. They are able to invest themselves completely in projects and people because they do not fear failure or rejection. Of course they suffer hurt and disappointment, but their setbacks neither damage nor diminish them. Owing to their resilience, they are open to growth experiences and relationships, tolerant of risk, quick to joy and delight, and accepting and forgiving of themselves and others.

To wrap up, there is, of course, a kind of porosity between the seven types of love, which keep on seeping and passing into one another. For Plato, love aims at beautiful and good things, because the possession of beautiful and good things is called happiness, and happiness is an end-in-itself. Of all beautiful and good things, the best, most beautiful, and most dependable is truth or wisdom, which is why Plato called love not a god but a philosopher:

He whom love touches not walks in darkness.

18

Polyamory: a new way of loving?

So far, we seem to have assumed that love is a relationship between two people. In 2006, the term polyamory ('many loves') made an entry into the Oxford English Dictionary. Polyamory is the philosophy or state of being romantically involved with more than one person at a time, with the knowledge and consent of all parties involved. The focus is more on intimacy than on sex, and polyamorous relationships, while being romantic, need not be sexual.

The opposite of polyamory is monogamy, which, as discussed in Chapter 1, is uncommon among animals: among humans, monogamy came about relatively recently, largely for social and economic rather than moral or romantic reasons. At the same time, polyamory is not synonymous with polygamy, which, unlike polyamory, is culturally sanctioned and codified, and typically takes the form of polygyny, that is, polygamy in which a man has more than one wife.

Neither is polyamory synonymous with cheating, swinging, or free loving, since the focus is on intimacy and relationship building, with the knowledge and consent of all parties involved.

In fact, while some people see their polyamory as an identity or orientation, others see it more in terms of an ethical alternative to infidelity. Despite its ethical dimensions, polyamory is more stigmatized than cheating: cheating may threaten the system, but at least it operates from within it, whereas polyamory simply disregards it.

Polyamorous relationships can take many forms. They can, for example, be triads, or quads, maybe one couple with another. 'Polyfidelity' refers to a closed polyamorous relationship in which the parties agree to restrict themselves to one another, rather than take outside lovers. In some cases, there may be a primary couple with one or more secondary partners who are perhaps more distant or occasional, although this need not mean that they are any less loved. In other cases, one partner may have, or wish for, outside relationships, while the other may be content with just the primary relationship. This particular form of polyamory, on the part of just one partner, need not involve any bisexuality. The possibilities and permutations are endless. The partners of one's partner, who are not also one's partners, are referred to in the jargon as 'metamours', and it is in the spirit of polyamory that one treats them with courtesy and respect, as friends rather than enemies or rivals.

As well as being close to the natural state of humankind, polyamory has long been recognized as an alternative lifestyle in gay subculture, and is becoming more and more mainstream, driven by feminism and gay emancipation, and the fragmentation of families and communities. When it is an important part of someone's identity, polyamory is more an orientation than a lifestyle choice, leading to demands for legal recognition and protection for at least some forms of polyamorous relationship.

What are the attractions of polyamory? For a start, polyamory is less limiting: it allows for rewarding relationships with more than one person, without the need to abandon one relationship for another, or to forego potentially rewarding relationships. To love more than one person is not necessarily to love each person less, just as to love two children is not necessarily to love each child less. 'True love,' wrote PB Shelley (1792–1822), 'in this differs from gold and clay/ That to divide is not to take away.' Love is not finite like money or time, but grows in the giving.

Polyamory recognizes that some people's relational needs are best met by more than one person, and, conversely, relieves the pressure of having to meet all of another person's needs. By creating more space around a tired relationship, it can breathe new love and new life into the relationship.

Because polyamory is non-exclusive, existing relationships and friendships are less likely to be abandoned or neglected in favour of a single person, leading to a larger and stronger social network with more resources, skills, and perspectives to draw upon. Unlike with serial monogamy, there is less incentive to write off an older relationship—and, by extension, a part of our history and who we are—simply because a more exciting or convenient one has come along.

Needless to say, polyamory also has its drawbacks. From a young age, we are taught that true love is the love of just one person, who, in turn, is able to answer all our needs. The princess awaits her prince, and, once united, they live happily ever after. There is no question of another prince, and still less of a knight, squire, or lady-in-waiting. Given this state of affairs, and the stigma of polyamory, it may be hard to find people, or enough people, with whom to conduct polyamorous relationships. It may be that polyamory is better suited to gay couples and gay people more generally, since it is then much less likely to call upon bisexuality, which is not in everyone's repertoire.

The vast majority of people are naturally prone to possessiveness and jealousy. The princess does not await the prince, but *her* prince. A new relationship is full of enthusiasm and excitement (or, in the jargon, 'New Relationship Energy'), which can be tough on an existing partner. Jealousy can be even more of an issue if only half of a couple is polyamorous, while the other half merely tolerates, rather than embraces, it.

Polyamory demands time, energy, security, self-knowledge, emotional intelligence, and communication skills. Notwithstanding the stigma and lack of legal recognition, things can get pretty complicated, which can undermine the quality of the relationships and the very viability of the enterprise. Many people may not have the time, energy, or skills to manage much more than one relationship, and, of course, may not feel a need for more than one partner, if even that.

But even if we decide to reject polyamory for ourselves, there can still be much to gain from adopting a more fluid, flexible, and forbearing approach to relationships.

19

The philosophy of lust

For Paul the Apostle, the purpose of marriage is no higher than to contain lust: 'For I would that all men were even as I myself... But if they cannot contain let them marry: for it is better to marry than to burn.'

Lust can be defined as the passionate longing or desire for certain things such as food, money, power, and, above all, sex. There are many reasons to desire sex with someone, among others, to be close to her, to hold on to or manipulate her, to hurt a third party, to hurt ourselves, to make a child, or to gain some advantage such as money or security. With lust, however, sex is contemplated primarily for itself, or, to be more precise, for the pleasure and release that it could procure.

It is possible to seek out sex for itself without this desire being lustful: for it to be lustful, it has to be disordered, that is, inappropriately strong or inappropriately directed relative to the prevailing social norms. King David was undone by his lust for Bathsheba, and Bill Clinton, while still the most powerful man in the world, was almost impeached by his lust for a young White House intern. According to mediaeval lore, when Alexander the

Great found Phyllis (by some accounts, Alexander's wife) riding Aristotle like a horse around the garden, he exclaimed, 'Master can this be!' Quick on his feet, Aristotle replied, 'If lust can so overcome wisdom, just think what it could do to a young man like you.' In Dante's *Divine Comedy*, souls that have committed the sin of lust are blown around in a whirlwind that represents their lack of self-control. Since Dante's time, MRI scanners have revealed that the same area of the brain lights up in people experiencing lust as in addicts receiving their cocaine fix.

But it is not just that lust can sometimes be overpowering. For Arthur Schopenhauer, lust ultimately directs all human behaviour. This is certainly borne out by modern advertising, which seems mostly about suggesting that buying a particular product will help us to obtain the objects of our lust. In contrast, no one ever spends money to be taught restraint or virtue. It is sometimes said that everything is about sex, except for sex itself, which is about power. Even the Church, needing to express ecstatic communion with God, could do no better than to picture it in terms of an orgasm.

Schopenhauer, who was heavily influenced by Eastern traditions, drew attention to the misery that is likely to pour out of lust. In the Hindu *Bhagavad Gita*, Lord Krishna declares that lust, along with anger and greed, is one of three gates to *Naraka* or Hell. When Arjuna asks him by what one is impelled to sinful acts 'even willingly, as if engaged by force', he replies, 'It is lust only, Arjuna, which is born of contact with the material mode of passion and later transformed into wrath, and which is the all-devouring sinful enemy of this world… Therefore, O Arjuna, best of the Bharatas, in the very beginning curb this great symbol of sin—by regulating the senses, and slay this destroyer of knowledge and self-realization...' For the Buddha, lust, in the broader sense of coveting or craving, is at the heart of the Four Noble Truths, which run as follows:

1. Suffering (*dukkha*) is inherent in all life.
2. The cause of all suffering is lust.
3. There is a natural way to eliminate all suffering from one's life.
4. The Noble Eightfold Path is that way.

Lust, said the Buddha, is controlled or eliminated through attaining a higher consciousness. This idea also surfaces here and there in the Western canon, and the poet Charles Baudelaire (1821–1867) went so far as to suggest that the artist, who is consciousness personified, ought never to have sex: 'Only the brute is good at coupling, and copulation is the lyricism of the masses. To copulate is to enter into another—and the artist never emerges from himself.'

As well as being harmful to the subject, lust is harmful also to the object. Lust is the only appetite that is for a person rather than an object, but a person qua object rather than qua person, shorn of uniquely human attributes such as dignity and agency. The lustful person is not only unconcerned about the blossoming of the object of his lust (and, in some cases, the blossoming of the 'old' partner to whom he is being unfaithful), but will act against her best interests to feed his appetite, and with his appetite sated, discard her as 'one casts aside a lemon which has been sucked dry'. These acerbic words belong to Immanuel Kant, who asserted that a person should never be treated as a means to an end but always as an end in herself. It is perhaps in the nature of lust that it seeks to possess or 'have' the other, to incorporate and degrade the other by destroying her dignity and autonomy. In Kingsley Amis's novel *One Fat Englishman*, the protagonist says that, when it comes to sex, his aim is 'to convert a creature who is cool, dry, calm, articulate, independent, purposeful into a creature who is the opposite of these: to demonstrate to an animal which is pretending not to be an animal that it is an animal'.

Because it is so subversive and destructive, lust is, in the words of Shakespeare, 'a waste of shame'. So as to secrete that shame, many cultures magic up a male demon that lays upon sleepers to have sex with them. This incubus (and the less prevalent female equivalent, or succubus) is made to carry the blame for embarrassing nocturnal emissions, disturbing claims of adultery and abuse, and even unexplained children.

Another response to the shame of lust, and much more prevalent in our culture, is to disguise lust as romantic love. Contrary to lust, love is respectable, even commendable. We look on approvingly at a pair holding hands or hugging, but we look around for the police if they start acting out their lust. Love is the acceptable face of lust, but the love that is lust in disguise is even more perverse and destructive, and in that sense, even more shameful, than the lust that knows its game. How to tell lust and love apart? While lust is hasty, furtive, and deceitful, love is patient, measured, and constant. While lust is all about taking, love is all about sharing. While lust is all about using, love is all about building. Lust can lead to love, but it is a poor start and a poor basis, akin to choosing your favourite book by its cover.

Of course, there is nothing wrong with sexual desire *per se*, and none of us would be here without it. Sexual desire is a life force, to be enjoyed and even celebrated as in the orgies of old. But as with the wine, the problems start when it turns from servant into master. We must be ready to recognize unbridled lust for the blind and destructive force that it is. Unbridled lust is especially unseemly in the elderly, because, as the saying goes, there is no fool like an old fool.

Lust is hard to extinguish, but is more readily redirected. If a man is angry with his boss, he may go home and act out his anger by lashing out at his spouse, or he may instead run for 30 minutes on a treadmill. This second instance of displacement—running on the treadmill—is an example of sublimation, which is the channelling of unproductive or destructive energies into constructive or creative activities. As Baudelaire put it, 'the more a man cultivates the arts, the less randy he becomes.'

For Plato, lust is the first step on the ladder of love, and not to be shunned or shunted; for it is by indulging our lust that we are able to move beyond it. In that much, lust can be its own cure.

This chapter is adapted from the chapter on lust in *Heaven and Hell: The Psychology of the Emotions.*

20

The magic of masturbation

Some people who marry do so in part 'to contain'. But, for various reasons, many people end up in a sexless, or virtually sexless, marriage. Even if sex does take place, it may not be satisfying or satisfying enough. Sex surveys are notoriously unreliable, but the top complaint about marriage on Google is lack of sex, with 'sexless marriage' entered into the search box eight times more often than 'loveless marriage'. And then, of course, there are all those who are single, divorced, widowed, travelling, and so on. Many of these people have recourse to masturbation; but even within a fulfilling sexual relationship, masturbation is, if anything, more common still.

Masturbation, or onanism, is the stimulation, often manual, of the genitals for sexual gratification. Masturbation is depicted in prehistoric cave paintings and has been observed in many animal species. In Egyptian myth, the god Atum created the universe by masturbating, and every year the pharaoh of Egypt ritually masturbated into the Nile. In some traditional cultures, masturbation is a right of passage into manhood, although there are some groups, notably in the Congo Basin, that lack a word for the activity and are confused by the concept. Alternative and divergent sexual practices such as masturbation and same-sex love are associated with periods of peace and prosperity. In unstable times with high infant mortality, the spilling of semen may be perceived as unnecessary, extravagant, or wasteful: although ejaculation is a rite of passage for young men of the Sambia tribe in New Guinea, it is brought about by fellatio so that the semen can be ingested rather than spilt. The Ancient Greeks regarded masturbation as entirely normal, if more the province of the common man, since the elites had a duty to further the family line, and, beyond that, had slaves for their relief.

The Christian tradition adopted an altogether different view of masturbation, rooted in an obscure passage of the Book of Genesis. When God killed Er, Er's father Judah told his second son Onan to marry Er's widow Tamar and 'raise up seed' to his brother. But when he lied with Tamar, Onan spilt his semen on the ground— no doubt because he knew that fathering a son in his brother's line would have cost him the larger part of his inheritance. This displeased God, 'wherefore he slew him also.'

In his *Medicinal Dictionary* (1743), the physician Robert James, a friend of Samuel Johnson, wrote of masturbation that 'there is perhaps no sin productive of so many hideous consequences'. More subtly, in the *Metaphysics of Morals* (1797), Immanuel Kant argued that 'a man gives up his personality… when he uses himself merely as a means for the gratification of an animal drive.' In his influential treatise on education (1762), the philosopher and Romantic trailblazer Jean-Jacques Rousseau advised that a tutor should not leave his pupil the slightest opportunity to engage in masturbation:

Therefore, watch carefully over the young man; he can protect
himself from all other foes, but it is for you to protect him against
himself. Never leave him night or day, or at least share his room;
never let him go to bed till he is sleepy, and let him rise as soon as
he wakes ... If once he acquires this dangerous supplement he is
lost. From then on, body and soul will be enervated; he will carry to
the grave the sad effects of this habit, the most fatal habit which a
young man can be subjected to.

This seems to be a case of 'do as I say, not as I do'. In his *Confessions*
(1782) Rousseau divulges that he discovered masturbation in Italy,
returning 'a different person from the one who had gone there':

[There I] learnt of that dangerous means of cheating Nature,
which leads young men of my temperament to various kinds of
excesses, that eventually imperil their health, and sometimes their
lives. This vice, which shame and timidity find so convenient, has
a particular attraction for lively imaginations. It allows them to
dispose, so to speak, of the whole female sex at their will, and to
make any beauty who tempts them serve their pleasure without the
need of first obtaining her consent.

In the 19th century, Jean-Etienne Esquirol, an eminent psychiatrist
and physician-in-chief at the Salpêtrière Hospital in Paris, declared
in his classification of mental disorders (1838) that masturbation is
'recognized in all countries as a cause of insanity', and it is not until
as late as 1968 that it finally fell out of the American classification
of mental disorders. In 1972, the American Medical Association
pronounced it to be normal, but the guilt, shame, and stigma still
live on to blight people's lives. In 1994, the Surgeon General of the
United States Joycelyn Elders had to resign after opining, in the

context of preventing young people from engaging in riskier forms of sexual activity, that masturbation 'is part of human sexuality, and perhaps it should be taught'. More tragically still, in 2013, a 14-year-old American boy took his life after a classmate filmed him touching himself in the changing rooms.

There is no doubt that masturbation can present a problem if it becomes distracting or distressing, undermines relationships, or is carried out in public; but it does not make people go mad, blind, impotent, or anything else. On the contrary, masturbation is associated with a number of important benefits:

1. Pleasure and convenience. Upon being challenged for masturbating in the marketplace, the ancient philosopher Diogenes the Cynic replied, 'If only it were so easy to soothe hunger by rubbing an empty belly.' According to Diogenes, the god Hermes, taking pity on his son Pan, gave him the gift of masturbation, which Pan then taught to the shepherds. Masturbation has no need of special equipment, sexual intercourse, or even a partner. Although it is often looked upon as the poor relative of sexual intercourse, many couples engage in mutual masturbation, either alongside or instead of intercourse, to simplify, improve, or enrich their sexual lives and arrive at orgasm.

2. Fewer complications. Masturbation is safe as well as convenient. Unlike sexual intercourse, it is very unlikely to lead to pregnancy or sexually transmitted diseases such as human papilloma virus, chlamydia, gonorrhoea, syphilis, herpes, and HIV/AIDS.

3. Stronger, more intimate relationships. Contrary to the popular perception, there is, at least in women, a positive correlation

between frequency of masturbation and frequency of intercourse. People who masturbate more are more sexually driven, and mutual masturbation is likely to increase the frequency and variety of sexual contact. Both in the performance and in the observation, masturbation can teach partners about each other's pleasure centres, proclivities, and particularities. If one partner is more sexually driven than the other, masturbation can provide him or her with a balancing outlet.

4. Better reproductive health. In men, masturbation flushes out old sperm with low motility and reduces the risk of prostate cancer. If practiced before sexual intercourse, it can delay orgasm in men suffering from premature ejaculation. In women, it increases the chances of conception by altering the conditions in the vagina, cervix, and uterus. It also protects against cervical infections by increasing the acidity of the cervical mucus and flushing out pathogens. In both women and men, it strengthens the muscles in the pelvic floor and genital area and contributes to extending the years of sexual activity.

5. Faster sleep. Masturbation invites sleep by reducing stress and releasing feel-good hormones such as dopamine, endorphins, oxytocin, and prolactin. Orgasm in particular brings on a state of stillness, serenity, and sleepiness, sometimes called 'the little death' (Fr. *la petite mort*), which can usher in a deeper sleep.

6. Improved cardiovascular fitness. Masturbation is, in effect, a form of light exercise. Compared to regular exercise, it is more effective or efficient at reducing tension and releasing feel-good hormones. The muscles and blood vessels relax, improving blood flow and lowering heart rate and blood pressure. No surprise,

then, that there is an inverse correlation between frequency of orgasm and death from coronary heart disease.

7. Brighter mood and other psychological benefits. Masturbation reduces stress and releases feel-good hormones, which lift mood and reduce the perception of pain. It promotes better, more restorative sleep, locking in sleep's myriad benefits. It enables younger people in particular to explore their sexual identity and master their sexual impulses, leading to a happier, healthier sexuality, as well as greater self-awareness, self-control, and self-esteem. It offers an escape from the demands and limitations of reality, an outlet for the imagination in fantasy, and a medium for the memory in nostalgia. And it culminates in a transcending experience that unites mind with body and life in death.

21

Touch hunger

Convicted murderer Peter Collins died of cancer after 32 years in a Canadian prison. In that time, he became a champion of prison rights, and made a short film called *Fly in the Ointment* about a prolonged period that he spent in solitary confinement:

> *Somehow, I felt [my wife's] fingers on my leg. Shocked and excited, I opened my eyes only to realize it was a fly walking on me. I was greedy for human touch so I closed my eyes and pretended it was her fingers. I tried to stay perfectly still because I didn't want to frighten the fly off and be left alone.*

After that, Collins would bite his cheek and apply a mixture of his own blood and saliva onto his skin to attract the flies that had become his only source of living touch.

Owing to smaller household sizes, greater migration, higher media consumption, and longer life expectancy, people today are more corporally isolated than at any other time in human history. Just like we crave food when we are hungry, and crave sleep when we are tired, so we crave touch when we are lonely, for to be lonely is to be vulnerable. When someone is out of our orbit, we do not say that we are *out of sight*, but *out of touch*; and we feel that we ought to *reach out* and *make contact*. More than a mere superfluity or indulgence, human touch is, like food and sleep, a visceral need that is increasingly being met by third parties such as massage therapists and even professional cuddlers.

As a wine taster, I used to think that smell was the most neglected of our senses. But in our society touch is even more so. In the 1960s, Sidney Jourard, a psychologist at the University of Florida, observed the behaviour of couples in coffee shops around the world. He found that, in the space of an hour, couples in Puerto Rico touched each other 180 times. This compared to 110 times in Paris, just twice in Florida, and not at all in London. Jourard also found that French parents and their children touched three times more than their American counterparts.

The fear of touch in northern, Anglophone countries is deep-seated. In Victorian England and 19th century America, people took to the language of flowers, or floriography, to fly feelings that could not otherwise have flown. In a book on child rearing, first published in 1928, the eminent and influential American psychologist John B. Watson (he of Little Albert fame) advised:

> *Never hug and kiss [your children], never let them sit on your lap. If you must, kiss them once on the forehead when they say goodnight… In a week's time you will find how easy it is to be perfectly objective with your child and at the same time kindly. You will be utterly ashamed at the mawkish, sentimental way you have been handling it.*

Still today, many people flinch if the person returning their change accidentally brushes their hand. Generally speaking, the fear of touch is much greater in men. Touch is seen as soft and effeminate, and many men are keen to appear macho or at least masculine. With women, they worry that their touch will be interpreted as a sexual advance. With other men, they fear that it will raise questions about their sexuality, or that it will feel awkward, or that it will be rejected, or that they might enjoy it a little too much. With children, with many schools now operating a strict no-touch policy, they fear that it might raise suspicions of paedophilia. So with the exception of handshakes and the occasional awkward 'man hug', men must forego touch, especially warm, intimate touch, simply to reassure everyone, and perhaps also themselves, that they are decent, manly men.

As they take their first steps out of the warm embrace of their parents, boys might try to meet their need for touch through rough interaction with other boys. As they grow still older, they may, often out of sheer desperation, fumble into a relationship, putting all their physical needs into the hands of just one other ill-equipped person. This places a lot of pressure on their partner and relationship. It also reinforces the link, and ambiguation, between touch and sex. Our libido can be assuaged with our hand in a way that our craving for touch cannot: as every sex worker knows, many people who think they are hungry for sex are in fact hungry for skin. But it is possible to separate the two, even with people to whom we feel sexually attracted.

To undermine the taboos surrounding it, I'm going to build a positive case for touch. Touch is the most primitive of all the senses. It is the first sense to develop, and is already present from just eight weeks of gestation. With a surface area, in adults, of around two square metres, the skin is the largest organ in the body.

In a controversial experiment of the 1950s, the psychologist Harry Harlow offered maternally deprived infant Rhesus macaques a choice of two inanimate surrogate mothers made of wire and wood: one bare, and the other covered in cloth. The monkeys preferred the cloth-covered surrogate to the bare one, even when the latter was holding a bottle of food.

In 1994, the neurobiologist Mary Carlson, one of Harlow's former students, travelled to Romania with the psychiatrist Felton Earls to study the effects of severe deprivation on the *decretei* children who had been abandoned to understaffed orphanages. Typical findings included muteness, blank facial expressions, social withdrawal, and bizarre stereotypic movements, behaviours very similar to those of socially deprived macaques and chimpanzees. Recent studies have reinforced the developmental importance of childhood physical contact, which has been associated with, among others, better performance on cognitive and physical tests, a stronger immune system, and reduced aggression. All else being equal, premature infants that receive a course of massage therapy gain considerably more weight and spend less time in hospital.

In adults, the benefits of gentle touch include: reducing stress and protecting against future stress, lifting mood and self-esteem, strengthening interpersonal bonds, improving cognitive function, and boosting the immune system. These effects are mediated by hormonal changes, not least a lowering of the stress hormone cortisol and the release of the 'love hormone' oxytocin. The benefits of touch accrue to the giver just as much as to the receiver, for it is impossible to touch without also being touched: people who give out 'free hugs' in public places are, of course, also having their hugs returned. Even self-massage reduces stress levels, which probably explains why we are constantly touching ourselves: wringing our hands, rubbing our forehead, brushing our hair and scalp, stroking our neck and upper back, and so on. Even masturbation may be more about touch and stress than about lust itself: in a recent survey by Time Out New York, 39 per cent of office workers admitted to masturbating in the workplace—and that's just the ones who admitted to it.

Compared to children, adults are less dependent on touch, but older adults, who tend to be more alone, more vulnerable, and more self-aware, are likely to need considerably more skin contact than their younger counterparts. Therapy animals have become common in care homes, and, despite a lifetime of inhibitions, residents can be encouraged to hold hands or rub each other's shoulders.

Just as we use speech and gestures to communicate, so we use touch. Words can say, 'I love you', but touch can also say how and how much, and, at the same time, 'I respect you', 'I need you', and 'thank you'. For a long time, scientists somehow thought that touch served merely to emphasize a verbal message. But now it is clear even to them that touch can be the message, and that it can be more nuanced and sophisticated than either speech or gestures, and more economical to boot. What's more, touch is a two-way street; and a person's reaction to our touch can tell us much more than their words ever could. Finally, while words can lie, or be taken for granted, primal touch is difficult to either ignore or discount.

Touch can also serve to convince and motivate, so long, of course, as it is natural and appropriate. One study found that two-thirds of women agreed to dance with a man who touched her on the arm while making the request. When the man kept his hand by his side, his success rate fell by as much as half. Students who, upon returning a library book, had their hand brushed by the librarian reported higher levels of satisfaction with the library and life in general, even if they had not been aware of having been touched. NBA teams with players who touched one another more, for example, by high-fiving or hugging during a game, went on to win more games, with the more touchy players doing best. Students who had been touched by a teacher tended to participate more in class activities, patrons who had been touched by a waitress tended to tip her more generously, shoppers who had been touched by a store greeter tended to spend more time in the store, and so on.

As a psychiatrist, I try to shake hands with all my patients, and often use comforting touch in moments of distress—almost invariably to good effect. Touch relaxes the patient, makes her feel that she has been seen and heard, and builds a bond of trust. It makes her, and me, feel more human, and, as a result, I think, we remember each other.

22

The pain of loneliness/
the joy of solitude

*I have discovered that all the unhappiness of men arises
from one single fact, that they cannot stay quietly in
their own chamber.*

—Blaise Pascal

According to a recent study, many people prefer to give
themselves a mild electric shock than to sit in a room alone
with their own thoughts.

Loneliness can be defined as a complex and unpleasant emotional
response to isolation or lack of companionship. It can be either
transient or chronic, and typically includes anxiety about a lack of
connectedness or communality. The pain of loneliness is such that,
throughout history, solitary confinement has been used as a form
of torture and punishment.

More than just painful, loneliness is also damaging. Lonely people
eat and drink more, and exercise and sleep less. They are at higher

risk of developing psychological problems such as alcoholism, depression, and psychosis, and physical problems such as infection, cancer, and cardiovascular disease.

Loneliness has been described as 'social pain'. Just as physical pain has evolved to signal injury and forestall further injury, so loneliness may have evolved to signal social isolation and stimulate us to seek out social bonds. Human beings are profoundly social animals, and depend on their social group not only for sustenance and protection but also for identity, narrative, and meaning. Historically and still today, to be alone is to be in mortal danger of losing oneself.

The infant is especially vulnerable and dependent, and loneliness may evoke early fears of helplessness and abandonment. In later life, loneliness can be precipitated by the loss of any important long-term relationship. Such a split entails not only the loss of a single meaningful person, but also, in many cases, of that person's entire social circle. Loneliness can also result from disruptive life events, including even joyous ones such as getting married or giving birth; from social problems such as racism or bullying; from psychological states such as shyness, agoraphobia, or depression; and from physical problems that restrict mobility or require special care.

Loneliness is a particular problem of industrial societies. It affects all segments of society, but is most prevalent and protracted in the elderly. According to a poll carried out in 2017 for the Jo Cox Commission on Loneliness, three-quarters of older people in the U.K. are lonely, and more than half of those have never spoken to anyone about how they feel. A full 39 per cent of respondents agreed with the statement that 'sometimes an entire day goes past and I haven't spoken to anybody'. These stark findings may be explained by such factors as smaller household sizes, greater migration, higher media consumption, and longer life expectancy. Large conglomerations built on productivity and consumption at the expense of connection and contemplation can feel profoundly alienating. The Internet has become the great comforter, and seems to offer it all: news, knowledge, music, entertainment, shopping, relationships, and even sex. But over time, it stokes envy and longing, confuses our needs and priorities, desensitizes us to violence and suffering, and, by creating a false sense of connectedness, entrenches superficial relationships at the cost of living ones. Man has evolved over several millennia into one of the most social and interconnected of all animals. Suddenly, he finds himself apart and alone, not on a mountaintop, in a desert, or on a raft at sea, but in a city of men, in reach but out of touch. For the first time in human history, he has no material need, and therefore no pretext, to interact and form attachments with his fellow men.

We tend to think of lonely people as single people, confusing people who are lonely with people who are alone, and people who are alone with people who are single. But people who are single are not necessarily alone, and people who are alone are not necessarily lonely. Conversely, it is possible and even common to feel at our loneliest when completely surrounded by partner, friends, and family. Based on extensive research, Bella DePaulo of the University of California has argued that, in aggregate, single people are in fact more sociable, self-sufficient, and fulfilled than married people despite the disadvantages and discrimination that they are made to suffer. Many people choose to remain single, and some even choose to isolate themselves, or, at least, not to actively seek out social interaction. Such 'loners'—the very term is pejorative, implying as it does abnormality and deviousness—may revel in a rich inner life or simply dislike or distrust the company of others, which, they feel, comes with more costs than benefits.

Timon of Athens, who lived at around the same time as Plato, began life in wealth, lavishing money upon his flattering friends, and, in accordance with his noble conception of friendship, never expecting anything in return. When he came down to his last drachma, all his friends deserted him, reducing him to the hard toil of labouring the fields. One day, as he tilled the earth, he uncovered a pot of gold, and all his old friends came tumbling back. But rather than welcome them with open arms, he cursed them and drove them away with sticks and clods of earth. He publically declared his hatred of mankind and withdrew into the forest, where, much to his chagrin, people sought him out as some kind of holy man. Did Timon feel lonely in the forest? Probably not, because he did not believe that he lacked for anything: as he no longer valued his friends or their companionship, he could not have desired or missed them—even though he may have pined for a better class of man and, in that limited sense, felt lonely.

Broadly speaking, loneliness is not so much an objective state of affairs as a subjective state of mind, a function of desired and achieved levels of social interaction and also of type or types of interaction. Lovers often feel lonely in the single absence of their beloved, even when completely surrounded by friends and family. Jilted lovers feel much lonelier than lovers who are merely apart from their beloved, indicating that loneliness is not merely a matter of interaction, but also of the potential for or possibility of interaction. Conversely, it is common to feel lonely within a marriage because the relationship is no longer validating or nurturing us but diminishing us and holding us back. As the writer Anton Chekov (1860–1904) warned, 'If you are afraid of loneliness, do not marry.' More often than not, marriage results not merely or even mostly from a desire for the permanent companionship of a single person, but also and above all from an urge to flee from our lifelong loneliness and escape from our inescapable demons.

Ultimately, loneliness is not the experience of lacking but the experience of living. It is part and parcel of the human condition, and, unless a person is resolved, it can only be a matter of time before it resurfaces, often with a vengeance. On this account, loneliness is the manifestation of the conflict between our desire for meaning and the absence of meaning from the universe, an absence that is all the more glaring in modern societies which have sacrificed traditional and religious structures of meaning on the thin altar of truth.

So much explains why people with a strong sense of purpose and meaning, or simply with a strong narrative, such as Nelson Mandela or St Anthony of the Desert, are largely protected from loneliness regardless of the circumstances in which they might find themselves. St Anthony sought out loneliness precisely because he understood that it could bring him closer to the real questions and value of life. He spent 15 years in a tomb and 20 years in an abandoned fort in the desert before his devotees persuaded him to withdraw from his seclusion to instruct and organize them, whence his epithet, 'Father of All Monks' ('monk' and 'monastery' derive from the Greek *monos*, 'alone'). Anthony emerged from the fort not ill and emaciated, as everyone had been expecting, but healthy and radiant, and lived on to the grand old age of 105, which in the 4th century must in itself have counted as a minor miracle.

St Anthony did not lead a life of loneliness but one of solitude. Loneliness is the pain of being alone, and is damaging. Solitude is the joy of being alone, and is empowering. Our unconscious requires solitude to process and unravel problems, so much so that our body imposes it upon us each night in the form of sleep. During the daytime, certain people can deliver themselves from the oppression of others by entering into a trance state. This practice tends to be more common in traditional societies, although I have on occasion witnessed it in some of my patients. By removing us from the distractions, constraints, and opinions imposed upon us by others, solitude frees us to reconnect with ourselves and with the world and to generate ideas and meaning. For Nietzsche, men without the aptitude or opportunity for solitude are mere slaves because they have no alternative but to parrot culture and society. In contrast, anyone who has unmasked society naturally seeks out solitude, which becomes the source and guarantor of a more authentic set of values and ambitions:

> *I go into solitude so as not to drink out of everybody's cistern. When I am among the many I live as the many do, and I do not think I really think. After a time it always seems as if they want to banish my self from myself and rob me of my soul.*

Solitude removes us from the mindless humdrum of everyday life into a higher consciousness which reconnects us with ourselves and our deepest humanity, and also with the natural world, which quickens into our muse and companion. By setting aside dependent emotions and constraining compromises, we free ourselves up for problem solving, creativity, and spirituality. If we can embrace it, this opportunity to adjust and refine our perspectives creates the strength and security for still greater solitude and, in time, the substance and meaning that guards against loneliness.

The life of St Anthony can leave the impression that solitude is at odds with attachment, but this need not be the case so long as the one is not pitted against the other—as, unfortunately, it so often is. For the poet RM Rilke (1875–1926), the highest task of lovers is that each stands guard over the solitude of the other. In *Solitude: A Return to the Self* (1988), the psychiatrist Anthony Storr convincingly argues that:

> *The happiest lives are probably those in which neither interpersonal relationships nor impersonal interests are idealized as the only way to salvation. The desire and pursuit of the whole must comprehend both aspects of human nature.*

Be this as it may, not everyone is capable of solitude, and for many people aloneness will never amount to anything more than bitter loneliness. Younger people often find aloneness difficult, while older people are more likely, or less unlikely, to seek it out. So much suggests that solitude, the joy of being alone, stems from, as well as promotes, a state of maturity and inner richness.

This chapter is adapted from the chapter on loneliness in *Heaven and Hell: The Psychology of the Emotions.*

23

The ascetic alternative

For centuries, the monasteries have offered a different type of marriage: marriage to God. What are the history, significance, and appeal of that alternative tradition?

Broadly speaking, monasticism is the religious renunciation of worldly pursuits to fully devote oneself to spiritual work. It is an important feature of the Roman Catholic Church and Eastern Orthodox Church, and also, in substantially different forms, of Hinduism, Jainism, and Buddhism.

Pythagoras

In Europe, monasticism had a number of pre-Christian incarnations. As a young man, Pythagoras of Samos took the advice of Thales of Miletus and travelled to Memphis to take instruction from Egyptian priests. At the age of 40, in around 540 BC, he established a philosophical and religious community in Croton, Southern Italy, which admitted both men and women. Those in the community's inner circle adhered to a strict set of rules, forsaking personal belongings, assuming a mainly vegetarian diet, and observing long periods of silence. Music played an important part in their lives: they recited poetry, sang hymns to Apollo, and played on the lyre to cure diseases of body and soul. They believed that 'All is number', and, thus, that any number could be expressed as a ratio of integers. One day, or so it goes, the Pythagorean Hippasus of Metapontum discovered irrational numbers and had to be drowned for his efforts.

Plato

Some 150 years later, in 387 BC, Plato founded a school (technically a *thiasos*, or religious confraternity) of mathematics and philosophy in a sacred garden called 'Academia' after the legendary Attic hero Akademos. Those with the means took up residence in neighbouring houses, and those without resided with others. The school became known as the Academy, and Plato remained its head or scholarch until his death some forty years later. Among all the men, he admitted two women, Axiothea of Phlius and Lastheneia of Mantinea—although they did have to dress like men. Later Athenian schools inspired by Plato's example include Aristotle's Lyceum and Epicurus' Garden. Plato's Academy survived in one form or another for some 900 years before being shut down by the Christian emperor Justinian in 529, a date that is often cited for the end of classical antiquity.

Paul of Thebes and the early Christian hermits

St Paul of Thebes (c. 227–342) is commonly regarded as the first Christian hermit. He fled into the Egyptian desert in around 250 during the persecution of Decius and Valerianus, and lived for almost a century in a cave near a clear spring and palm tree. Early Christians moved into the wilderness either to escape persecution

or draw closer to God. In this, they followed the example of Old
Testament prophets such as Elijah and John the Baptist, and of
Christ himself, who fasted for forty days and nights in the Judaean
desert while being tempted by Satan. In Matthew 19, Jesus says
that 'there be eunuchs, which have made themselves eunuchs
for the kingdom of heaven's sake'. He counsels: 'If thou wilt be
perfect, go and sell that thou hast, and give to the poor, and thou
shalt have treasure in heaven...'

Anthony

It is said that St Anthony the Great (c 251–356) met with Paul in
around 342, conversing with the 113-year-old hermit for one day
and one night. As a young man, Anthony spent 15 years in a tomb,
resisting the temptations and torments of the devil—an episode
that has often been depicted in art, including by modernists such
as Cézanne and Dalí. He then spent 20 years in an abandoned
fort in the desert before other hermits coaxed him out to instruct
and organize them. Although the hermits still lived separately,
they came together on Sundays to worship and break bread. *The
Life of Anthony* by the near contemporary bishop St Athanasius of
Alexandria inspired many to seek out the monastic life.

Pachomius

In around 323, St Pachomius the Great brought some hermits
together at Tabennisi in Upper Egypt, thereby creating the first
coenobitic (Gr. *koinos bios*, 'common life') monastery. The hermits,
or monks, each had their own hut or room, but shared a common
space for praying, working, and eating, under the authority of an
abbot or abbess (Aramaic, *abba*, 'father'). Pachomius established

several such communities, including some for women, opening up the spiritual life to those lacking the physical and mental constitution to survive alone in the desert.

Basil and the Eastern tradition

Influenced by Pachomius, St Basil the Great (329–379) founded monasteries in Cappadocia in modern-day Turkey. The moderate Rule of St Basil, or *Ascetica*, set the model for Eastern Orthodox monasticism. Another important treatise in the Eastern tradition is the Ladder of Divine Ascent (*Scala Paradisi*), composed by St John Climacus in around 600: this consists of thirty parts or 'steps' pointing to the highest religious perfection. John Climacus headed the monastery on Mount Sinai, built by Justinian to enclose the Chapel of the Burning Bush. The monastery, now St Catherine's Monastery, contains the world's oldest continuously operating library. Over in northeastern Greece, the traditions of the Autonomous Monastic State of the Holy Mountain (Mount Athos) stretch back to the 8th century. Mount Athos is home to twenty monasteries and over two thousand monks under the direct jurisdiction of the Ecumenical Patriarch of Constantinople, Bartholomew I, the 270th holder of the title. Although technically part of the European Union, the free movement of people and goods is prohibited, and only men can enter.

Monasticism in the West

After Constantine legalized Christianity in 313, it became the principal Roman religion, with violent persecution giving way to ascetic deprivation as a means of martyrdom. In the West, monasticism began by imitating the Egyptian model. In around

361, St Martin of Tours established a hermitage near Poitiers, now called Ligugé Abbey, after the Latin for 'small hut', *locaciacum*. In around 388, St Augustine of Hippo with some friends founded a lay ascetic community in Thagaste, North Africa, to be re-founded, centuries later, as the Augustinian Order. In 415, inspired by his travels in Palestine and Egypt, St John Cassian built a 'double monastery', later the Abbey of St Victor, in Marseille, with complexes for both men and women.

Benedict

John Cassian's *Conferences of the Desert Fathers*, consisting of interviews with 24 Egyptian monastics, exerted a strong influence on St Benedict of Nursia (480–543/7), who is regarded as the father of Western monasticism. Benedict lived for many years as a solitary hermit in a cave at Subiaco, near Rome. He became the abbot of a nearby monastery but proved unpopular with the monks, who may have tried to poison him. Later, he founded several monasteries around Subiaco, and, in around 529, the great monastery of Monte Cassino between Rome and Naples. The moderate Rule of St Benedict, with its almost equal emphasis on prayer and work (*ora et labora*), set the pattern for monastic rules across Europe, and, more than 1,400 years later, remains the most commonly adopted rule.

Celtic monasticism

Celtic monasticism, which flourished in Ireland in the 5th to 7th centuries, resembled Egyptian monasticism in its rigour and mysticism: even the Celtic cross with a circle in the middle appears to derive from Coptic Egypt. In the Irish Church, abbot-bishops administered the faithful along tribal, rather than territorial, lines. The strong emphasis on learning preserved Greek and Roman texts and culture on the fringes of a continent in chaos, and a zeal for itinerant missionary work led to the evangelization of large parts of the British Isles. Aside from St Patrick, who is regarded as the founder of Christianity in Ireland, important figures include St Columba (521–597), who founded Iona Abbey in Scotland; St Aiden (590–651), who founded Lindisfarne Priory in Northumberland; and St Columbanus (543–615), who founded several monasteries including Luxeuil Abbey in France and Bobbio Abbey in Italy. It has been said that, whereas the Rule of Saint Benedict taught people to become good monks, the rules of the Celtic monasteries taught people to become saints. The Rule of St David (500–589), the patron saint of Wales, stipulated that monks should drink only water and eat only bread, and pull the plough themselves. David and his followers came to be known as the Watermen, owing to their taste for water, and their custom of reciting the 150 psalms while standing up to their neck in an icy river.

Anchorites

From the earliest days, an alternative to being a hermit or monk was to become an anchorite, withdrawing from the world by being walled up into a cell, or anchorhold. The committal service contained elements of a funeral rite, with the anchorite becoming something of a living saint. Typically, the anchorhold was built against a church, with a window opening into the church to listen to services, receive the Eucharist, and dispense spiritual advice to visitors. There were also two other windows: one for light, and the other for food, drink, and other necessities. Most anchorites were anchoresses, the most famous being Julian of Norwich

(1342–1416). Her *Revelations of Divine Love* is the first book in English to have been written by a woman.

Monastic orders

Most early monasteries, both in the East and West, had around 12 members. In later times, some monasteries housed hundreds of monks and became important landowners. In 1098, a group of Benedictine monks founded Cîteaux Abbey to the south of Dijon, with the aim of returning to the literal observance of the Rule of St Benedict. In 1113, St Bernard of Clairvaux joined Cîteaux with 30 companions, and, over the years, greatly expanded the Cistercian Order. But over the decades and centuries, many Cistercian monasteries relaxed their habits. In the 17th century, another reform movement began at the Abbey of la Trappe in Normandy, giving rise to the Cistercians of the Strict Observance, or Trappists.

More austere still is the Carthusian Order, founded by St Bruno of Cologne in 1084. Unlike the Cistercians and Trappists, the Carthusians are not a branch of the Benedictines, but follow their own Rule, called the Statutes. Each charterhouse encloses a 'community of hermits', with each monk eating, working, sleeping, and praying in his own cell—much like the early monks of Egypt. The Carthusian Motherhouse in the Chartreuse Mountains near Grenoble is noted for the liqueur Chartreuse, made from distilled alcohol aged with 130 herbs, plants, and flowers.

Active orders

In contrast to the above 'contemplative' orders, of which there are many more, 'active' orders are immersed in mainstream society, seeking to reach out rather than remain remote and cloistered, with the balance between action and contemplation varying from one community to another. Because active orders do not aim at self-sufficiency, they usually live off the generosity of others, making them so-called mendicant ('begging') orders. Adherents of mendicant orders like the Franciscan, Dominican, and Jesuit orders are called friars (Lat. *frater*, 'brother') rather than monks.

The Franciscans (greyfriars) are a group of related mendicant orders established in 1209 by St Francis of Assisi, who sought a return to the source by emulating the example of Jesus. Franciscans generally follow the example of their founder, radical at the time, of wandering, preaching, and begging, although some communities are more focused on contemplation.

Like the Franciscans, the Dominicans (Order of Preachers, blackfriars, jacobins) committed themselves to making faith more relevant to the people. But unlike the Franciscans, they sought to achieve their aims by preaching the Gospel and combating heresy. Founded in the France of 1216 by St Dominic of Caleruega, the order is renowned for its intellectual tradition, and can boast several eminent thinkers, not least Albertus Magnus (1200–1280) and Thomas Aquinas (1225–1274), the *doctor angelicus*. The religious orthodoxy and intellectual dexterity of the Dominicans put them at the forefront of the Inquisition: punning on their name, people dubbed them the 'Hounds of the Lord' (*Domini canes*).

Founded in the France of 1540 by soldier-turned-mystic St Ignatius of Loyola, the Jesuits (Society of Jesus) are colloquially referred to as 'God's soldiers'. The order emphasizes education,

missionary evangelism, and obedience to the papacy. It does
not require members to live strictly in community, giving them
more latitude to travel and labour 'for the greater good of God'
(*Ad maiorem Dei gloriam*). The teaching dispensed in the order's
many schools and universities is broad and liberal, and the Jesuits
also run spiritual retreats—St Ignatius being the author of the
influential *Spiritual Exercises*. With a presence in 112 countries,
the Jesuits are one of the largest groups in the Roman Catholic
Church. As missionaries, they played an important role in the
Counter-Reformation, but have generally stood on the margins
of Church hierarchy. Pope Francis is, notoriously, the first Jesuit
Pope.

Benefits of monasticism

Setting aside the religious and spiritual dimensions, monasticism
served a number of important social functions. After the fall of
the Western Roman Empire, the monasteries helped to preserve
important texts, and education and culture in general. They also
created culture by their highly disciplined monks and nuns, and as
great patrons of art, music, and architecture. To this day, university
life is modeled on the monastic ideal, with quadrangles and
cloisters, communal meals, dormitory residences, and elaborate
robes and rituals. For centuries, the monasteries provided refuge
from war, famine, and disease, and served as outlets in particular
for the younger sons of aristocratic families, celibates, and other
misfits. In their drive for self-subsistence, they contributed to
the development of agriculture and manufacturing, for example,
turning viticulture and winemaking into fine arts. It is only in
modern times that the state superseded the monasteries in the
provision of social services such as health and education. But above

all, monasticism enabled, and still enables, people to live alone together, and to lead thoughtful, mindful lives with few of the distractions of the temporal world.

Criticisms of monasticism

Critics on the other hand have argued that monasticism involves an unnatural degree of self-abnegation for which there is little or no biblical basis. It creates a certain image of the virtuous life, congenial to some but not to others, whereas the virtuous life can take any number of forms. It creates a hierarchy of believers, and demands subordination to that hierarchy: for some of its adherents, it is little more than a form of 'holier-than-thou' vanity. By promoting celibacy and sequestration, it undermines family and society; and with its tendency to decadence, it can grow parasitic on the local community. Monasticism is not a feature of Islam, Zoroastrianism, or the Baha'i Faith. In Europe, movements such as the Protestant Reformation, the English Reformation, the French Revolution, and the Spanish Civil War led to the dissolution and destruction of many monasteries.

Monasticism today

Western monasticism has long been in decline, with growth in Asia and Africa unable to offset reductions elsewhere. In contrast, Eastern monasticism has been undergoing something of a revival, especially in the territories of the former Soviet Union. Even in Europe and America, monasticism continues to attract interest as an alternative way of life. The diverse New Monasticism movement seeks to translate monastic customs and insights into forms that are better suited to the modern world: communities are typically ecumenical, with a focus on contemplation, community, and charity, but without the traditional vows of celibacy, poverty, and obedience.

24

Are married people healthier?

There is research to suggest that married people are more likely to survive cancer, less likely to suffer a stroke or heart attack, less likely to develop depression and other mental illnesses, and the list goes on.

The health advantage of marriage seems small but significant, roughly equivalent to that of a healthier diet or regular exercise. According to one study, compared to single people, married people are 14 per cent more likely to survive a heart attack, and ready to be discharged from hospital two days sooner.

Interestingly, men seem to benefit from marriage more than women, perhaps because married women tend to be in a subordinate position, or tend to be more affected by marital conflict. In at least one study, single women fared almost as well as their wedded counterparts. Also, older couples seem to benefit considerably more from marriage than younger ones, probably, and in large part, because older people tend to be more vulnerable and therefore more dependent.

The health advantage of marriage is generally ascribed to better social support. A spouse is likely to encourage healthier habits and provide emotional and practical support in times of need. She or he is likely to be in the vicinity in the event of an emergency, if only to dial an ambulance. In addition, married people are more likely to have health insurance, and less likely to engage in risky behaviours such as substance misuse or dangerous driving. And, of course, they enjoy the social approval and recognition that come with marriage.

Rather than marriage promoting health, it may be that health promotes marriage, that is, that people with better health and more resources are more likely to get or remain married. But it appears that the health advantage of marriage persists even after controlling for such factors.

Of course, one need not be married to enjoy the benefits of companionship. Non-marital cohabitation appears to confer a similar health advantage. Single people may depend on relatives, friends, and colleagues, while at the same time having fun with their dates. They may also own a dog, cat, or other pet. Pet ownership has been associated with some of the same benefits as marriage, including better mental and cardiovascular health—and one might wonder which of marriage or pet ownership provides the greater benefit. Perhaps it depends on the pet.

Both marriage and pet ownership have been found to lower levels of the stress hormone cortisol, which can impair immune function. Cuddling, or even just interacting, with a spouse or pooch releases the 'love hormone' oxytocin, which promotes feelings of calm and closeness. In contrast, the feeling of loneliness is both unpleasant and damaging (Chapter 22).

On the other hand, people in unhappy marriages may feel more stressed and unsupported than most single people, to say nothing of those married people with an abusive spouse or going through the trauma of a divorce. Divorce is one of the most stressful of all life events. Beyond middle age, divorced people, even if they have remarried, are actually in *worse* health than people who have never married.

But all these are just averages and statistics, and there may be much more to them than meets the eye. Everyone is different, and all marriages are different. Matrimony may be a great boon if you are the marrying type, and if you can manage to remain happily married. But the Dalai Lama never married, and he's in pretty rude health.

25

The deep psychology of the bachelor party

If a man decides to get married, the first thing he might do is throw a bachelor party. A bachelor party is an initiation into marriage, which, in modern times, is mostly understood as a celebration, by the groom's male friends, of the groom's last days of 'freedom'. In the U.K., it tends to be called a stag (stag night, stag do, stag party…), and in Australia, a buck. The equivalent rite for the bride, attended by the bride's female friends, is the bachelorette or hen party.

The original meaning of 'bachelor' in English is 'a young knight who follows the banner of another'. 'Stag' and 'hen' used to be slang for 'man' and 'woman'. The stag, standing proud and alone, has long been a symbol of virility, with stags, and men with antlers, being a common motif in cave paintings. Cernunnos, the Celtic god of life and fertility, and a symbol of the masculine, featured the body of a warrior and the horns of a stag. The stag's horns, which point to the gods above, serve to attract mates and fend off rivals: mirroring the cycle of life and death, they grow and fall back each year, transmutating from soft, pulsing velvet into hard horn.

Although their modern forms are fairly recent, the stag and hen party derive from immemorial customs. In Ancient Greece, a bride joined her female relatives and friends in paying tribute to Artemis, goddess of childbirth and protector of young girls. In Sparta, friends marked the groom's last night of freedom with a banquet. It is possible that, by marrying six times, the party-loving Henry VIII embedded the banqueting tradition into England. For a long time, stags involved a formal dinner hosted by the groom's father or best man, or, for the more humble, a simple drink among friends.

From the late 19th century, a 'hen party' referred to any gathering of women. The term appears to have acquired its modern meaning in the 1960s and 70s. It first appeared in *The Times of London* in 1976, albeit in quotation marks, in the context of a male stripper fined by Leicester Crown Court for acting in 'a lewd, obscene and disgusting manner'. Back then, the bride often celebrated with her co-workers, whom she would be abandoning for the life of housewife and mother. In time, hen parties spilt out into nearby pubs and clubs, increasingly mirroring stags.

A rite of passage such as marriage marks a transition from one sphere to another, attended by an important change in social status. According to the ethnographer and folklorist Arnold van Gennep, rites of passage have three ritual phases: separation, transition, and incorporation. Separation rituals, such as the matriculation ceremony upon entering university or the crew cut upon joining the military, symbolize detachment from a former life. In France, the bachelor party is called *enterrement de vie de garçon*, which literally means 'burial of the life of the boy'. In modern stags, the separation ritual often involves stripping or humiliating the groom.

134

Western culture lacks formal rites of passage for adulthood. In other cultures, these typically feature tests of virility or maturity, which, in the West, tend to be subsumed into the stag or hen, often in the form of an alcohol endurance test or an activity such as archery, hammer throwing, or bungee jumping. Bungee jumping also represents a leap and separation; it is, in effect, a symbolic suicide.

In many traditional societies, the separation ritual for marriage involves initiating the bride into the duties of marriage, including lovemaking and childbearing—a function which in our culture has largely been delegated to the stripper, if not a sex toy or pornography. This reveals an important function of the rite of passage, which is to guide and support us at a difficult and critical time in our life.

Another possible function of the separation ritual for the bride is purification. In Orthodox Judaism, the bride immerses herself in a ritual bath, or *Mikveh*. In many Eastern traditions, the bride wears henna dye in intricate patterns, most commonly on her hands and feet, for decoration, purgation, and protection. In Germany, the bachelor party is called *Junggesellenabschied* ('farewell to bachelorhood'), but there is a separate event called *Polterabend* on the night before the wedding: in a tradition that stretches back to pre-Christian times, guests at a *Polterabend* break old crockery to drive out evil spirits. The modern heir to all of these traditions is, of course, the spa day.

Other, more minor functions of the stag and hen may include:

- Poking fun at marriage to make it seem less threatening.
- Snatching the groom back from the bride's grasp, and vice versa.

- Punishing the bride and groom for forsaking their friends.
- Saluting one's friends.
- Saying goodbye to one's friends.
- Tying in one's friends for the future.
- Creating a pretext to spoil oneself or one's friends.
- Creating a pretext for socially sanctioned release and debauchery—not dissimilar to the orgy (Chapter 7).
- Celebrating the life of the groom or bride.
- Celebrating manhood or womanhood.
- Inducing social conformity.

In the space of a generation, hens and especially stags have evolved into elaborate affairs involving various degrees of drunkenness and debauchery, often over several days in some faraway city of sin. The gatherings have spawned an entire industry, with event planners offering activities such as paintballing and tank driving, and supplying everything from dare lists to drinking games, and stretch-limousines to strippers breaking out of tiered cakes.

Why have stags and hens grown so important? From an economic standpoint, travel has become cheap and commonplace. People are marrying later and earning more, leaving them with more disposable income than ever before. From a sociocultural standpoint, our generation is more liberated, and perhaps more self-indulgent, than previous ones. The stag in particular may represent a frenetic attempt to express deep-rooted but increasingly threatened ideas about masculinity—and, indeed, about marriage itself.

For most of human history, marriage stood as an inescapable familial, social, and economic imperative. But in recent years, with falling infant mortality, rising life expectancy, and increasing gender equality, it has become more and more of a lifestyle choice. Inevitably, part of the bride or groom is unsure about tying the knot, and the stag or hen is, at some level, a manic defence against a loss of freedom and possibility; and, for the other revellers, against the loss of yet another friend to what can seem like an increasingly arcane and remote institution. The purpose of the manic defence is to prevent feelings of fear and sadness from rising into the conscious mind by distracting it with opposite feelings of euphoria and purposeful activity. In Virginia Woolf's *Mrs Dalloway*, one of several ways in which Clarissa Dalloway prevents herself from thinking about her life is by planning frivolous events and then preoccupying herself with their prerequisites—'always giving parties to cover the silence.'

26

Should we have a big wedding?

With the stag and hen over, it's time to start planning the wedding ceremony.

According to a survey by The Knot, in 2016, the average cost of a wedding in the U.S. shot up to over $35,000. But weddings have not always been such lavish affairs.

For most of the history of the Catholic Church, people could, and did, marry simply by saying so. There was no specific formula or ritual, and they did not need the authority of a priest or the permission of their parents—although in practice, especially in the upper classes, families often arranged the marriage or, at least, approved of the partner. Some people got married at the church door, sometimes with the blessing of the parish priest—whence the elaborate porches that still adorn some older English churches. But many tied the knot on a hill or cliff or other beauty spot, down the pub, at home, at a crossroads, or pretty much anywhere.

It is only in 1184, as part of a move to condemn the Cathars, that the Council of Verona decreed marriage to be a sacrament alongside baptism, confirmation, eucharist, penance, anointing of the sick, and holy orders. (Broadly speaking, the later Protestant tradition does not conceive of marriage as a sacrament and, as a result, has been more accepting of divorce.) In 1215, the Fourth Lateran Council headed by Pope Innocent III required couples to announce their intention to marry, or 'cry the banns', so that any impediments to their marriage could be voiced. The *Tametsi* decree, issued in 1563 by the twenty-fourth session of the Council of Trent, called for the presence of the parish priest or his delegate along with at least two more witnesses. But many regions did not follow *Tamesti*, and it is not until the *Ne Temere* decree, issued in 1907 by Pope Pius X, that the canonical form of marriage with a church minister and two witnesses became a universal requirement.

So when in all this did the white dress come in? Traditionally, brides simply wore their best dress to their wedding. White dresses, being impossible to clean, were beyond the means of most. In any case, the colour of purity in those days was not white but blue—which is why the Virgin Mary is usually portrayed in blue. White wedding dresses only became fashionable during the Regency, and popular after Queen Victoria wore one to marry Prince Albert in 1840.

The tradition of putting the bridesmaids into matching dresses is much older, going back to Roman times when it served to confuse the evil spirits threatening to curse the bride. Also protecting Roman brides from evil spirits was the bridal veil, which also symbolized the virginity and modesty of the bride. Traditionally, the father or groom lifted the veil at the time of the kiss to reveal the bride as the groom, almost literally, took her into his possession. Like the dress, the veil has grown into an overblown status symbol.

For luck, the bride would wear, as per the opening line of a Victorian rhyme: 'something old, something new, something borrowed, something blue'. These four items represented, respectively, the bride's family and her past, her future, borrowed happiness, and virtue. At the wedding of Prince William and Catherine Middleton, the bride wore Carrickmacross lace as something old, a pair of diamond earrings from jewellers Robinson Pelham as something new, one of the Queen's tiaras as something borrowed, and a ribbon sewed into her dress as something blue.

Historically, the bouquet held by the bride consisted of herbs like garlic and rosemary to ward off evil spirits. Rather than posies, flower girls, or their equivalents, carried sheaves of wheat to symbolize fertility. At her wedding, Queen Victoria opted for fresh flowers and, of course, flowers caught on. After the wedding, the bride tosses the bouquet over her shoulder into a crowd of unmarried women, and the one to catch it is said to be next in line for marriage.

Owning a piece of the wedding dress brought good luck, and wedding guests would rip the bride's dress to shreds as they led the newlyweds to their bedchamber. This developed into the tradition of the groom removing a garter from the bride and tossing it into a crowd of braying bachelors, both to keep them at bay and as proof of consummation. The man who caught the garter would put it onto the woman who had caught the bouquet, and, perhaps, begin to court her.

The wedding ring goes back at least to Ancient Egypt, where the circle was a symbol of eternity. It is placed on the fourth finger, the *annularis*, because the Egyptians believed that the principal vein in that finger, the *vena amoris*, runs straight to the heart. In 1549, Edward VI of England decreed that the ring should be worn on the left hand, where it has remained ever since. Upon their betrothal in 1477, Maximilian of Austria gave Mary of Burgundy a diamond ring, popularizing the diamond ring among the upper classes—long before the extremely successful De Beers 'A diamond is forever' marketing campaign, which took off in 1948. In that period and at least until the Reformation, the betrothal ring, rather than the wedding ring, was the primary ring associated with marriage. The practice of having an engagement period may have arisen out of the Fourth Lateran Council of 1215 and the crying of the banns; but, before that, the betrothal and wedding rings would have been one and the same. For a long time, only women wore wedding rings, and, in England, upper class men such as Prince William still do not.

At the wedding, the ring is often carried by the best man. Once upon a time, the best man assisted the groom in capturing the bride from her kinsmen: to this day, the groom stands to the right so that his sword hand is free to fend off any assailing in-laws.

The Egyptians tossed rice or grain at weddings to underwrite the fertility of the couple, but the wedding cake itself comes to us from the Roman era, when, for fertility, guests would tear a loaf of bread over the bride's head. Wedding guests in mediaeval England brought along small cakes, which they stacked up for the newlyweds to kiss over—a practice which inspired the French *croque-en-bouche* cake. Queen Victoria's 300-pound wedding cake was covered in pure white sugar, which was very expensive, and, like the white wedding dress, became a means of flaunting one's wealth and status. Sugar rationing did not end until

1953, but, still, the Queen's wedding cake in 1947 stood nine-foot tall and weighed 500 pounds. After the wedding ceremony, it was served up at a celebratory 'breakfast' (lunch) at Buckingham Palace.

Only in the late 19th century did people begin to hold weddings in the afternoon—often in the month of June, named for Juno, the Roman goddess of marriage and wife of Jupiter. June is also the season for the harvesting of honey: in Ancient Rome and a number of other cultures, after the wedding, the bride drank honey mead or honey wine every day for one moon to help her fall pregnant. The modern 'holiday' honeymoon dates back to the *Belle Epoque*, before the Great War put a damper on jollies to the French and Italian rivieras.

The exorbitant cost of the modern wedding owes to a combination of factors, among which the rise of romantic love, egalitarianism, and the Internet, with people playing prince and princess before the altar and then having the pictures posted to their social media streams. At the same time, marriage is morphing into a middle class and middle age institution, with the poor and young, who would have had simpler weddings, increasingly opting for cohabitation or singledom (Chapter 31).

If we do have a wedding, should we have a big one? According to a recent study, high wedding attendance is positively associated with marriage duration—as is having a honeymoon, regardless of its cost. So far, so predictable: but the study also found that marriage duration is inversely associated with spending on the engagement ring and wedding ceremony. In particular, brides who spend $20,000 or more on their wedding are 3.5 times *more likely* to divorce than those who spend half that amount. So, yes, we should have a big wedding, but not an expensive one.

27

The challenges of intimacy

The next three chapters—on intimacy, trust, and forgiveness—look at some of what it takes to make marriage, or any relationship, work, or work better.

Emotional intimacy can be understood as a state of closeness between two people resulting from a process of interaction through which they feel able to share increasingly sensitive and significant aspects of themselves that they normally keep hidden, in some cases, even from themselves.

It begins with one person taking a risk by disclosing a private, personal, and emotionally charged thought, feeling, or biographical detail that leaves him or her exposed and vulnerable, in the hope or expectation of a supportive response, which, if forthcoming, encourages further self-disclosure from both parties. This process is largely dependent on trust, which, in the absence of a strong pull factor such as mutual physical attraction, can take years to build.

Intimate discourse need not be verbal, and can also take the form of emotional expressions, meaningful glances, sustained eye contact, physical proximity, touch, and such like. Emotional intimacy can lead to physical intimacy, and, albeit less commonly, physical intimacy to emotional intimacy. As a result, the two are sometimes confused. Historically, human beings lived in large families in tightknit communities that provided for all kinds of intimacy. But today, many people rely on just one person, usually their romantic partner, for all their intimacy needs, reinforcing the notion that one cannot have emotional intimacy without physical intimacy, or that they are one and the same thing. Intimacy exists on a spectrum, and in different shapes and forms: it is possible to create some degree of intimacy in all our relationships, even the most formal or fleeting ones, and it may be that our most intimate relationship is not with our spouse or sexual partner.

Compared to men, women are much better at creating intimacy, meaning that a woman's most intimate relationship is often with a same-sex friend. In general, men guard their privacy more closely than women. They are more reluctant to self-disclose, especially to other men. Interestingly, this is not, or not as much, the case for men from non-Western societies, suggesting that the problem has more to do with culture than with any biological differences between men and women. In the West, men are taught to associate emotions, emotional sharing, and emotional warmth with effeminacy and homosexuality; and to value macho traits such as assertiveness, autonomy, and resilience which conflict with naked self-disclosure. As a result, men prefer to reveal themselves in fits and starts, usually under the cover of some other activity such as drinking or sports.

This is a great loss for the male sex. Intimacy can feel like a bubble of bliss in which, at last, we are able to be ourselves, and, more than that, affirmed in ourselves. Tapping into the perspective, experience, skills, and resources of another person broadens our horizons and increases our possibilities. Their unconditional support makes us feel stronger and more secure. Their interest and participation in the minutiae of our experience seems to enrich it, lending texture and substance to our otherwise mundane, almost mechanical lives. Unsurprisingly, people who report having one or more intimate relationships tend to be happier and healthier, and intimacy is an important predictor of long-term relationship satisfaction.

Given its promise, the ability to create and sustain intimacy is central to a certain kind of flourishing life. Deep intimacy depends upon healthy self-esteem, to tolerate the vulnerability that comes from the self-disclosure of emotionally charged material. It also calls for courage and curiosity and a fair amount of self-knowledge, with many avenues for further intimacy sealed off by not knowing what one thinks or feels, and, more to the point, not wanting to find out. It is, of course, not just about scrutinizing ourselves but also about reading the other, reaching beyond their words to arrive at their true meaning and adapting our every interaction so that it accords with their, and our own, perspectives, dispositions, and sensitivities.

Intimacy involves both give and take, often at the same time within the same interaction; and people who are narcissistic or otherwise self-obsessed should take care not to confuse friendship with an onslaught of one-sided 'self-disclosure'. Intimacy cannot be imposed upon people. Nor can it be forced out of them, for example, by probing too soon or too directly into their deepest secrets. It has to come naturally, gradually, at its own pace, if it is not to undermine the very trust upon which it is built. It can take a long time to start seeing someone for the person that they truly are, rather than as an object or instrument in our world. It is impossible to trust someone who seems to be coming at us with an agenda of their own and scant regard for our needs, sensibilities, and particularities. Modern dating, which is mostly about instant gratification, and largely depends upon matching a certain profile or stereotype, can leave us feeling like little more than a hologram, or else a lump of flesh at the meat market.

Once achieved, intimacy isn't necessarily the sinecure that we might have hoped for, particularly if the affection that follows in its train has acquired the existential flavour which people generally call love. Inevitably, life follows its course, with competing priorities and attachments taking their toll on the relationship. Having poured so much of ourselves into the other, we become painfully sensitive to the slightest sign of disdain or indifference on their part, which we interpret as a loss of their goodwill and, more than that, an indictment of the person that we are—and which they know so well. Our natural reaction is then to snipe back or pull up the drawbridge, further undermining the connection that took so long to establish. Later, we may change tack and tighten our grip, and, suddenly, like a bar of soap, our relationship slips out between our fingers. On both sides, affection turns into anger, trust into resentment, and friendship into enmity.

What we forgot is that intimacy has a life of its own, that it cannot be forced or imposed, and that, sometimes, the best way to save a relationship is to step back before it is too late.

28

The philosophy of trust

What is trust, when does it pertain, and can it ever be absolute?

In Book 2 of Plato's *Republic*, the character of Glaucon, who is in conversation with Socrates, argues that most people are fundamentally self-interested, but maintain a reputation for virtue and justice to evade the social costs of being or appearing unjust. But if a man could get hold of the mythical Ring of Gyges and make himself invisible, he would most surely behave as it suited him: "No man would keep his hands off what was not his own when he could safely take what he liked out of the market, or go into houses and lie with any one at his pleasure, or kill or release from prison whom he would, and in all respects be like a god among men." We behave justly not because we value justice, but because we are weak and fearful; while the unjust man who is cunning enough to seem just will get the better of everyone and everything.

As part of his lengthy reply to Glaucon, Socrates famously conjures up an idealized Republic to help him 'locate' (define) justice, first in the state and then in the individual. Socrates argues that justice and injustice are to the soul as health and disease are to the body: if health in the body is intrinsically desirable, then so is justice in the soul. For Socrates, an unjust man cannot be happy because he is not in rational and ordered control of himself.

Even if Socrates is right and justice is intrinsically desirable, people with the ring of Gyges on their finger, or even without, may still choose to behave unjustly. If people no longer fear for the consequences of their actions, if they have little or nothing to lose, we can no longer rely on them; and if we can no longer rely on them, they can no longer rely on us. Trust breaks down, with each defending against the other, and even attacking the other to pre-empt an attack. The state falls into turmoil, enabling the most violent, ruthless, and devious to rise up like the scum on an angry sea. But even their tyranny will be short-lived. In *The Prince* (1532), his instruction manual for aspiring princes and tyrants, Machiavelli warns that 'victories are never so clear that the winner does not have to have some respect, especially for justice'.

In the *Nicomachean Ethics*, Aristotle maintains that man is made good either by nature, or by teaching, or by habit. Nature, he says, is not in our hands, and few people heed the voice of reason. All that remains is habit, and most of what passes for virtue is no more than automaton custom and habit. Ultimately, good habits arise from good laws, and, in that much, justice begets justice.

The English philosopher Thomas Hobbes was born prematurely when his mother heard of the approach of the Spanish Armada. As Hobbes later put it, 'my mother gave birth to twins: myself and fear.' In his masterpiece *Leviathan* (1651), Hobbes argues that the absence of laws, trust, and peace, which he calls the state of nature, is so abhorrent to men that, through a combination of fear and reason—but mostly fear—they come together to cooperate. In a memorable line, Hobbes characterizes the life of man in the state of nature as 'solitary, poor, nasty, brutish, and short'.

For Hobbes, peace and cooperation are best achieved by a social contract establishing a commonwealth, a giant body politic—or leviathan—with an absolute sovereign at its head. For the sake of self-preservation, people agree to divest themselves of certain rights, restricting their liberty to that which they would tolerate in others. The sovereign's role is to enforce the contract, which, owing to human nature, is under constant threat. Like the human body, leviathan is prone to disease and deformity. The general inclination of mankind, says Hobbes, is 'a perpetual and restless desire of power after power, that ceaseth only in death'.

Game theory helps to explain why two rational people might not cooperate even when cooperation is in their best mutual interests. In the archetypal prisoner's dilemma, two gang members are arrested and entered into solitary confinement. The prosecutors offer the prisoners a bargain. Each prisoner can either testify against the other, or cooperate by remaining silent. If both remain silent, they serve just one year in prison. If both testify against the other, they serve two years in prison. If only one testifies against the other, he is freed and the other serves three years in prison (and vice versa). Whether or not the other cooperates, it is better to grass on him; and the same, of course, is true for him. But the equation changes if the prisoners know that their gang kills defectors, or if they believe that they will have to work together again. If marriage promotes trust and goodwill, it is also because both parties know that they cannot easily escape from each other's clutch. In the words of Hobbes, 'covenants without the sword are but words…'

Assuming that our gang kills defectors, I could rely on my colleague in the other cell to cooperate, but does that mean I trust him to cooperate? If I rely on others not to attack me because they are minimally rational and it is in their interest not to break the social contract, does that mean I trust them with my wellbeing, or even that I trust them not to attack me? If a stranger robbed me, I would feel upset but not betrayed, and betrayal is the counterpart of trust. In other words, Hobbes thinks so little of human nature that he cannot even conceive of genuine trust, and, by his social contract, offers us no more than a pale imitation.

Happily, human nature is a bit brighter than Hobbes surmised. People are not cold, calculating machines that sometimes break down, but cooperative animals equipped with social feelings such as love, compassion, shame, and guilt. Such feelings may help, but it is entirely possible to rely on someone's love without also trusting her, while trusting people, such as doctors and judges, who clearly do not love or even sympathize with us.

Instead, trust is established when I ask or allow a suitable candidate to take at least some responsibility for something that I value, thereby making myself vulnerable to her, and she agrees to take that responsibility, or, in the circumstances, can reasonably be expected to do so. I trust my doctor with my health because, by virtue of being a doctor, and my doctor, she has taken some responsibility for my health—and, of course, I have asked or allowed her to do so. But even then, my trust in my doctor is not all-embracing: given the kind of person that she is, and the nature of our compact, I can trust her with my health, but not, say, with my finances.

My doctor may well one day decide, for one reason or another, to stop caring for my health, but I would expect her to regretfully make me aware of this fact, and maybe to make transitional arrangements so as to protect the thing that I value and entrusted her with, in this case, my health. If she withdrew herself in this measured and considerate manner, I would feel sad, disappointed, and perhaps annoyed, but I would not feel betrayed, or, at least, not nearly as much I would otherwise have.

The French for trust is *confiance*, which, like the English 'confidence', literally means 'with faith'. Perhaps we cannot trust people not to let us down, other than by a leap of faith similar to belief in God, with the length of the leap determined by such factors as fear, habit, nature, reason, and love. But we can just about trust them—or some of them—not to mislead us, and to let us down lightly.

29

The philosophy of forgiveness

Forgive me
Is all that you can't say
Years gone by and still
Words don't come easily
Like forgive me forgive me

—Tracy Chapman, *Baby Can I Hold You*

In June 2017, five men were jailed for their part in a failed attempt to break into the wine cellar of famed collector Michel-Jack Chasseuil, who was threatened with a Kalashnikov rifle and had some of his fingers broken during the terrifying ordeal. Chasseuil commented: *Je pardonne mais je n'excuse pas*—'I forgive but I do not excuse what they have done.'

What did Chasseuil mean by this? What is the difference between forgiving and excusing? The definitions are open to contention, but to forgive is essentially to make a conscious effort to overcome justified anger or resentment, and associated negative emotions such as vengefulness, stemming from an offensive deed or situation. To excuse on the other hand is to seek to lessen the moral blame attaching to the offence with the aim of exonerating the perpetrator. So Chasseuil probably meant that, while he had overcome his negative feelings towards the men, this did not imply that they were any less culpable or deserving of punishment. Some have argued that to forgive is to forbear punishment, but Chasseuil's stance suggests that forgiveness and punishment need not be at odds.

Other concepts related to forgiveness include condoning, tolerating, pardoning, and mercy. If to excuse is to seek to lessen the moral blame attaching to an offense, to condone is to deny that there is any blame in the first place by disregarding or discounting any negative judgement and attendant resentment. To tolerate, at least in the moral sense, is to acknowledge the blame but live with it. To pardon is to write off an offense on the grounds that it was involuntary. A pardon is also a legal and political concept exercised by a third-party authority, such as the President of the United States, to absolve a person convicted of a crime, who must in turn accept the pardon. Mercy is compassion and leniency for someone whom it is in our power to punish or harm. In a judicial context, mercy, or clemency, is, as John Locke put it, 'the power to act according to discretion, for the public good, without the prescription of the Law, and sometimes even against it.'

Compared to forgiving, which is typically although not invariably for a particular instance, condoning and tolerating have more to do with patterns of behaviour; and while it is possible to condone or tolerate blameworthy actions that are directed at others, we can only properly forgive those blameworthy actions that are directed at ourselves. Moreover, it is not the actions themselves that we forgive so much as the person who committed them, saying something like, "I forgive *you* for". Much more than condoning or tolerating, forgiving belies the moral relationship between self and other, which it aims at rebalancing. If I say, "I forgive you," I am implying that you have wronged me (or at least that I think or feel that you have wronged me), and placing you in my debt. But if you do not accept that you have wronged me, you may yourself feel wronged by my forgiveness—and so sometimes, for minor offences, it may be more judicious to keep our forgiveness to ourselves, that is, to behave like we have forgiven but without actually saying so.

Genuine forgiveness is not the overcoming of resentment by any means, or else one could forgive by losing one's memory, but implicates a kind of moral process. By the end of this process, the victim should have been able to forswear revenge, moderate or let go of resentment, and rehabilitate the offender by reframing their relationship as one of moral equals. Of course, this process, which is at the heart of forgiveness, is greatly eased by the cooperation of the offender. The offender should seek to divest himself of his bond of guilt by going through a reciprocal process of taking responsibility for the offensive deed, accounting for it, repudiating it, and committing not to repeat it or anything like it—since the fear of further offense is a significant impediment to forgiveness. From an emotional standpoint, he ought to empathize with the plight of his victim and express and experience remorse. Given enough time, forgiveness need not require the cooperation of the offender, who may be unrepentant, unreachable, or dead.

Historically, an offender may also have submitted to a formal apology ritual, which served to bring forth forgiveness by upholding or reasserting the dignity of the victim in forgiving.

In January 1077, the Holy Roman Emperor Henry IV trekked
to Canossa Castle in Reggio Emilia to obtain the revocation
of his excommunication from Pope Gregory VII. Gregory had
excommunicated Henry for demanding his abdication, but now
Henry needed the revocation to save his crown. Before granting
the revocation, Gregory made Henry wait outside the castle on his
knees for three days and three nights, while a blizzard raged on.
Henry's penance enabled Gregory to grant the revocation without
losing his dignity or looking like a pushover. Centuries later, the
German Chancellor Otto von Bismarck coined the expression 'to
go to Canossa', which means 'to submit willingly to humiliation'.
The modern equivalent of the apology ritual, depending on the
severity of the offense, is perhaps to offer a bunch of flowers or box
of chocolates, or to make dinner.

By rebalancing the moral relation between self and other,
forgiveness enables us to move on with our lives, not only by
repairing our relationships but also and above all by ridding us
of the resentment or guilt that blinds us to our bigger picture. In
addition, forgiveness reinforces important values such as mutual
respect, accountability, and peace. Forgiveness is a major theme in
Leo Tolstoy's *War and Peace* (1869): Princess Marya forgives her
father, Natasha forgives Anatole Kuragin, Prince Andrei forgives
Natasha, Pierre forgives Dolokhov. None of it is easy, but by rising
to forgiveness these characters grow in themselves and in our
hearts, while characters like Countess Rostova and Prince Nikolai
Bolkonsky are brought down by their resentment and inability to
forgive or ask for forgiveness.

But, for all that, should we always forgive? There may be certain
offenses, such as the violent murder of a relative, that truly are

unforgivable. But even if everything can be forgiven, forgiveness might not serve the best interests, particularly when the offender has not made amends, or enough amends. In this case, to forgive the offense is to leave it unpunished, and, more than that, to condone, and therefore invite, the bad behaviour of which it is an instance; whereas to withhold forgiveness is to signal that the offense is both grave and inadmissible, and to pressure the offender into reconsidering his stance and reforming his attitude while at the same time reaffirming our values and upholding our dignity. Even if raw resentment has been overcome, it might be judicious to withhold forgiveness as a kind of moral protest, or for prudential reasons. This suggests that there is more to forgiveness than the mere overcoming of resentment.

Interestingly, classical thinkers like Plato and Aristotle did not share in our concept of forgiveness as a means of overcoming justified anger or resentment, nor did they consider forgiveness as one of the virtues. For them, a virtuous person is immune from moral harm by lesser persons, and therefore has no need of forgiveness. In Plato's *Apology*, Socrates tells the jurors that his accusers, Meletus and Anytus, will not injure him: "they cannot; for it is not in the nature of things that a bad man should injure a better than himself."

In the *Nicomachean Ethics*, Aristotle says that actions are either voluntary, in which case they attract praise or blame, or involuntary, in which case they ought to be (to use the most accurate term) pardoned. Significantly, actions that are voluntary—*prima facie*, most actions—are not to be pardoned, because, being voluntary, they are not pardonable. But neither should they give rise to undue anger, which, being a form of intemperance, is opposed to reason, and therefore a vice. Anticipating modern moralists such as Immanuel Kant—who, along with Christianity, is largely responsible for the concept of people as moral equals—the Roman Stoic Seneca thought of anger as a vice because, through anger, we see others as less than fully human. At the end of his trial, Plato's Socrates says: "I am not angry with my accusers, or my condemners; they have done me no harm, although neither of them meant to do me any good; and for this I may gently blame them."

In the *Rhetoric*, Aristotle defines anger as an impulse, accompanied by pain, to a conspicuous revenge for a conspicuous slight which betrays the offender's opinion that the victim is obviously of no importance. Aristotle says that people are more prone to anger if they are insecure or in some form of distress such as poverty or love; and one can easily imagine him arguing that, because the virtuous person is above the offender's opinion, he has no reason to be angry. Anger, says Aristotle, can be quelled by the feeling that the slight is deserved, by the passage of time, by the exaction of revenge, by the suffering of the offender, or by being spent on someone else (an early insight into the ego defence of displacement). But, significantly, the Master of Those Who Know, as Dante called him, makes no mention of forgiveness as a means of redress.

Like Greco-Roman notions of forgiveness, the concept of forgiveness in the Bible has more to do with pardon than with an overcoming of resentment. The Greek word *aphiemi*, which in the Bible is sometimes translated as 'forgiveness', literally means 'to let go or release, as of a debt or bond'. In Leviticus 16, God instructs Moses and Aaron to sacrifice two goats every year. The first goat is to be killed, after which the High Priest is to lay his hands upon the head of the second goat and confess the sins of the people. In Leviticus 16:10, the word *aphiemi* is used in the context of the second goat, or scapegoat, as it is sent forth into the wilderness with its burden of sin. The sacrifice prescribed in Leviticus, symbolized by the altar in the sanctuary of every church, prefigures that of Jesus, who played the role of the first goat in his human crucifixion, and that of the second goat in his divine resurrection. Upon seeing Jesus for the first time, John the Baptist exclaimed, "Behold the Lamb of God, which taketh away the sin of the world!"

In Christianity, to forgive is to abandon our claims against others, just as God abandoned his claims against us, sending out our sins 'as far as the east is from the west'. 'Let all bitterness, and wrath, and anger, and clamour, and evil speaking, be put away from you, with all malice: And be ye kind one to another, tenderhearted, forgiving one another, even as God for Christ's sake hath forgiven you.' To forgive is not merely to imitate God, but to have him imitate us: 'For if ye forgive men their trespasses, your heavenly Father will also forgive you: But if ye forgive not men their trespasses, neither will your Father forgive your trespasses.' In Christian ethics, forgiveness is a manifestation of love: our love for others is an echo of God's love for us, and the greatest expression of that love is in forgiveness.

These notions come together in the parable of the prodigal son in Luke 15. The younger of a man's two sons asks for his inheritance—which, note, almost amounts to wishing the man dead. He then sets off for a faraway land, where, in a fantastic turn of phrase, he 'wastes his substance with riotous living'. Having worn down his inheritance, he becomes a swineherd, and envies the swine for the husks that they eat. With famine in the belly, he resolves to return to his father and plead to be taken in as a servant. But instead of spurning him, the man falls upon his neck and kisses him. The elder son walks into the homecoming feast and begrudges the man for killing a fatted calf for his dissipated brother, while he, ever obedient, never found any such favour from his father. But the man counters that it is right that they should make merry: 'for this thy brother was dead, and is alive again; and was lost, and is found.'

Ancient notions of forgiveness may seem inadequate or incomplete, but manage to sidestep an important problem with the modern concept of forgiveness as the overcoming of resentment. The problem is that resentment, or the kind of resentment that ought to be overcome, is necessarily inappropriate, leaving forgiveness with no intrinsic moral worth. If people have no free will and no meaningful control over their actions, resenting them can serve no more than an instrumental purpose aimed at shaping their behaviour. If they do have free will and their actions fall short, they deserve our measured resentment. But if they make the right amends, our resentment is no longer appropriate, and 'forgiveness' requires no special effort. If, on the other hand, they do not make the right amends, resentment remains the right or moral response: to forgive them in these circumstances would be to imply that our resentment was inappropriate or excessive, and therefore vicious. Ultimately, virtue is not a matter of forgiving but of being appropriately and at the same time detachedly resentful; or, if free will does not exist, or not much, pretending to be.

30

The rise and demise of divorce

According to the Office for National Statistics, between 1970 and 1993, the number of divorces per thousand married women in England and Wales rose from 4.7 to 14.1. But between 1993 and 2014, it fell back to 9.3. In 1993, there were 165,018 divorces and 299,197 marriages in England and Wales; in 2014 there were 111,169 divorces and 247,372 marriages.

According to the National Center for Family and Marriage Research, the divorce rate in the U.S. rose from 14.9 per thousand married women in 1970 to a peak of 22.8 in 1980. It subsequently fell back to 16.9 per thousand in 2015, a fall of 25 per cent since 1980.

Here are seven reasons for the overall increase in the divorce rate:

1. Divorce is easier to obtain. In the 16th century, Henry VIII of England had to break from the Catholic Church to do away with Catherine of Aragon and marry Anne Boleyn. Prior to 1857, divorce in the U.K. called for an Act of Parliament. In 1858, there were just 24 divorces in England and Wales; in 1900, there were 512. Until as late as 1971, divorce usually required proof of fault,

such as adultery, abandonment, cruelty, or intoxication. Between 1971 and 1972, the number of divorces in England and Wales leapt from 74,437 to 119,025. In 1970, California became the first U.S. state to introduce no-fault divorce.

2. Women are more independent. Women have better rights, including under divorce law. More and more women are financially independent. If they are unable to support themselves, they can claim welfare from the state. All this means that they are in a much better bargaining position. In the U.K., wives petition about two-thirds of divorces, and generally obtain the better settlement.

3. Divorce is more socially acceptable. With the increasing secularization of society, marriage is seen more as a social contract than a sacrament. In the past, couples often stayed together for the sake of the children; but today, many people take the view that, by removing them from conflict, divorce can actually be good for the children.

4. Divorce breeds divorce. Studies have found that: compared to first marriages, second and subsequent marriages are more likely to end in divorce; couples in reconstituted families are more likely to get divorced; and children with a divorced parent are more likely, one day, to get divorced. Other risk factors for divorce include: coming from very different backgrounds; knowing each other for a short time before marriage; young age; poor educational attainment; financial strain; addiction to alcohol or drugs; sexual promiscuity; misaligned sex drives or other sexual incompatibility; and disagreement about whether or not to have children (Chapter 32).

5. People are living longer. Between 1970 and 2015, life expectancy in the U.K. rose from 72.0 to 81.6 years, which is about double the life expectancy in 1841. People now have much longer in which to fall out or grow apart, and it has become much harder to wait for death to do the job of divorce.

6. People have unrealistically high expectations of marriage. In the past most people married for pragmatic reasons, or because they had no choice. Today most people marry for romantic love, and expect the romance to last. But people are flawed and fallible, and love comes and goes.

7. We live in a consumerist culture. Our society is more individualistic and materialistic than any that went before. We tend to focus on what we lack instead of being grateful for all that we already have. When something is torn or broken, we don't bother to mend or repair it: we just throw it out and replace it with a new one. And, inevitably, we begin to take the same attitude with our relationships.

Here are five reasons for the more recent fall in the divorce rate:

1. People are waiting longer to get married. Between 1974 and 2014, the average age of marriage in England and Wales rose from 28.8 to 37.0 for men and 26.2 to 34.6 for women. Young age is a risk factor for divorce.

2. People are waiting longer to have children, and having fewer of them. In England and Wales, the average age of mothers at the birth of their child rose from 26.7 to 30.3 years between 1970 and 2015. In the same period, the fertility rate fell from 2.44 to 1.83 in

the U.K., and from 2.48 to 1.86 in the U.S. Fewer children later puts less strain on a marriage.

3. People are more isolated than ever before. A U.S. study found that, between 1985 and 2004, the proportion of people reporting having no one to confide in almost tripled. In 1985, respondents most frequently reported having three close confidants; by 2004, this had fallen to none. People with no one to fall back on may be less likely to leave their marriage.

4. Fewer people are getting married (Chapter 31). Cohabitation and singledom are more socially acceptable, while marriage has become something of a lifestyle choice. Many jurisdictions offer alternative forms of civil union, such as the Civil Solidarity Pact (PACS) in France or Civil Union in New Zealand. The share of children born outside of marriage increased in the EU-28 from 27.3 per cent in 2000 to 42.0 per cent in 2015. In 2015, extramarital births outnumbered births inside marriages in several E.U. member states, including France, Sweden, and Portugal. People who choose marriage over its alternatives are probably better suited to it, and to their partner.

5. Marriage is becoming a middle class institution. Analysis of Census 2011 data by the Marriage Foundation uncovered that 79 per cent of all parents in social class AB are married, compared to just 37 per cent of parents in social class DE. People who are skilled, affluent, and from similar backgrounds are less likely to get divorced.

In conclusion, the fall in the divorce rate may seem like a very good thing—and in some respects of course it is. But in reality, divorce is falling because marriage is dying—or, at least, dying as a universal institution.

31

The future of the family

The family is the link between the individual and society: changes in family structure and composition are driven by social change, and, at the same time, drive social change—which is why sex and marriage have been, and still are, so tightly controlled and regulated.

Historically, certainly in Catholic Europe, the primary purpose of getting married and founding a family was to produce a legitimate male heir. Adultery, especially on the part of the wife, was severely sanctioned, and, although the Church did not recognize divorce, a marriage could be annulled on the grounds of impotence or infertility.

In those days, marriage was, as it still is in some cultures, a social alliance, with little or none of the romance or sexual compatibility that drives modern marriages. Still today, the family invites reproduction, while at the same time regulating sexual function, and providing a structure and medium for the free flow of economic, human, and cultural capital. It harnesses strong human instincts to socialize and empower the next generation, and to meet, as best as it can, the physical and psychological needs of all its members, for shelter, for care, and for love. In general, the family performs these tasks better than the state, and at lesser cost. It is, at its best, the ultimate safety net.

The model of the family that is most often in the media consists of a white, heterosexual couple with two healthy, happy children living together under the same roof. The man and the woman in this cereal packet family are in a marriage built upon a still on-going romance between two stereotypes. The man is the main breadwinner, and, *in extremis*, the decision-maker and disciplinarian. He is the 'head of the family'. Meanwhile, the woman devotes herself to the home and children. If she works, the man's career takes priority. The man and the woman support and complement each other. They invest every spare resource into their children, which, in turn, attest to their high status and good character.

The cereal packet family is the archetype of the nuclear family with a couple and their dependent children. The other main type of family is the patrilocal extended family, characterized by co-residence with or near the man's family. Extended families used to be much more common, although, at least in pre-industrial Britain, late marriages and low life expectancies prevented them from outnumbering nuclear families. The nuclear family grew in prestige and pre-eminence after the Second World War as the workforce became more mobile and specialized agencies took over many of the traditional functions of the extended family, in particular education, healthcare, and welfare.

But in more recent decades, the nuclear family, and especially the cereal-packet family, has come under increasing strain.

Women are more empowered than ever before, and are often the main breadwinner in the family, with the male partner staying at home as a househusband or establishing a relationship of equals. More people are putting passion and fulfilment above compromise and stability, leading to serial monogamy, which is no longer stigmatized. Voluntary childlessness is more common, and developments in reproductive technology are creating more options for those who want to have children outside of a more traditional arrangement. At the same time, economic forces such as rising tuition fees and property prices, and a retreat of the welfare state, are shifting responsibility back onto the family, including the extended family, which, supported by rising life expectancies and easy travel and communication, is making something of a comeback.

According to the Office for National Statistics (ONS), in 2016, there were 18.9 million families in the U.K. These included 12.7 million married or civil partnered couples (of which 4.8 million had dependent children), 3.3 million cohabiting couples (of which 1.3 million had dependent children), and 2.9 million lone parent families (of which 1.9 million had dependent children). Of all families with dependent children, 45 per cent had one child, 40 per cent had two, and 15 per cent had three or more.

In the twenty years from 1996 to 2016, the number of cohabiting couples more than doubled. Many cohabiting couples function like married couples in all but name. Other forms of cohabitation include the 'trial marriage' (which, if things work out, leads to marriage) and the short-term or uncommitted relationship. In many cases, cohabitation serves to delay marriage while the couple establishes a financial foothold.

In the same twenty-year period, the number of lone parent families rose by some 20 per cent. In the past, the parent in a lone parent family was likely to have been widowed by war, childbirth, or disease. Today, the lone parent is far more likely to be separated or divorced—and, owing to shifting social attitudes and developments in reproductive technology, more and more people are electing to bring up children on their own. A lone parent may eventually re-partner, sometimes with another lone parent, to form a reconstituted family.

Same-sex couple families accounted for one per cent of all couple families: 87,000 same-sex couple families were cohabiting, 47,000 were in a civil partnership, and 29,000 were married. 14,000 same-sex couple families had dependent children. These children may have come from a previous relationship or through other opportunities such as adoption, artificial insemination, or surrogacy. In the year to 31 March 2016, same-sex couples in the U.K. adopted 450 children, or 9.6 per cent of the total number of children adopted in that year. Most researchers in the field agree that children raised by one or two gay or lesbian parents suffer no particular disadvantage.

Interestingly, over the decade to 2016, multi-family households grew by 66 per cent to 323,000, or 1.2 per cent of all households. This could owe to a combination of higher life expectancies and higher property prices pushing young adults with a family to move into a parent's home, or invite the parent to live in theirs. Alternatively, multi-family households could consist of unrelated families sharing a household, perhaps in a more central or convenient location than they could otherwise have afforded. With a rising number of dual-earner households and lone-parent families, more and more grandparents are being relied upon for childcare or financial support. Many grandparents welcome this new role in life, but some do resent it, particularly if they also have to care for their very elderly parents.

Many families are 'empty nest' families, with grown-up children who have left the family home. However, there is a trend for emancipated children to bounce back into their old bedroom. In 2016, 25 per cent of young adults aged 20 to 34 were living with their parents, up from 21 per cent in 1996. Of note is that a substantial majority of these boomerang children are male. While some parents are delighted by the return of a prodigal son, others feel imposed upon, particularly if their grown-up child is indolent, disruptive, or outright abusive, or a drain on the family finances.

According to the ONS report, as many as 7.7 million people were living alone. 28 per cent of households contained just one person, up from 17 per cent in 1971. The majority (54.2 per cent) of people who lived alone were women, partly because women have a higher life expectancy than men, and partly because they tend to have married men older than themselves. But within the age group of 16 to 64, the majority (57.7 per cent) of those living alone were men. This could be because more men than women never marry; because men marry at a later age than women; or because, after a split, children are much more likely to remain with their mother. Of the 1.9 million lone parent families with dependent children, a full 90 per cent were headed by a woman.

Not all people who live alone are single: some 10% of all adults in the UK are 'living apart together' (LAT), with each partner in the relationship maintaining or living in a separate household. Some people who LAT have little choice in the matter; for others, it is a first step to cohabitation or, especially for older people, a happy compromise between intimate companionship and autonomy.

In the end, the cereal packet family contained the seed of its own destruction. Today more than ever, people are chasing romance and, in the process, creating instability. High divorce rates over the years have led to a considerable number of lone parents and reconstituted families. Assisted by rising life expectancies, economic and social forces are shifting responsibility back onto the extended family, and, at the same time, helping to ease an epidemic of loneliness among the elderly. Younger people are choosing cohabitation over marriage, and it is possible to envisage a looser form of cohabitation overtaking marriage, along with a more serial or task-driven approach to partnering over the course of a lengthening lifespan. The relation between man and woman is increasingly one of equals, although it is very apparent from lone parent families in particular that women are still doing the bulk of the childrearing. More and more people are choosing a childfree life, or having children outside of a more traditional arrangement, and both these trends seem set to continue. It is still early days for same-sex relationships, which may grow more common as gender and sexuality become more fluid and relationships less beholden to old stereotypes and an imperative for procreation.

32

Should we have children?

Despite not having any himself, Pope Francis has said that we ought to have children:

> *A society with a greedy generation, that doesn't want to surround itself with children, that considers them above all worrisome, a weight, a risk, is a depressed society ... The choice not to have children is selfish. Life rejuvenates and acquires energy when it multiplies: it is enriched, not impoverished.*

In that much, Pope Francis is merely echoing scripture. Psalm 127 tells us that 'children are an heritage of the Lord: and the fruit of the womb is his reward'. In the Book of Genesis, the very first thing that God says to man upon creating him is, 'be fruitful and multiply, and replenish the earth...'

In most times and places, the only lasting impact that a woman could make was to bring forth children. She would have been married off at a young age, and would seldom have exerted much choice or control over her reproductive life. Things changed dramatically over the last century with the advent of women's rights and reliable contraception. Owing to the state pension and social support, people no longer have to rely on having children to safeguard their old age. And childlessness is much less stigmatized than it used to be—and even praised in certain circles. In 2012 in England and Wales, around one in five women at the end of their childbearing years (women born in 1967) had never had children, compared to just one in nine women in their mothers' generation (women born in 1940). The more a woman is educated, the less she is likely to have children. For many women, children conflict with work; whereas for men, children may well mean working more than they would otherwise have had to. But here's the rub: in the long run, people with children and people without report being similarly satisfied with their lives.

Another factor in the rise of childless, or childfree, women is the decline of marriage. Many people equate marriage with children, and being unmarried is one of the strongest predictors of childlessness. In 1980 in England and Wales, the fertility rate among married women was almost five times as high as that among unmarried women: in 2016, it was still almost twice as high. In 1980, only 12 per cent of babies were born outside of marriage, compared to 48 per cent in 2016—although two-thirds of that 48 per cent were born to cohabiting parents.

Children tend to fare better if they are raised by two parents, and fare best if the parents are married. Marriage generally offers more stability and resources. Children raised within a marriage are much less likely to suffer physical or sexual abuse. They tend to be in better health, to do better at school, and to have fewer emotional and behavioural problems. This may have as much to do with the kind of people who get married as it does with marriage itself. People who will make better parents, or who have more resources, are more likely to tie the knot; and, as discussed in Chapter 30, marriage is fast becoming a middle class preserve.

Before examining some of the main arguments for and against having children, it is worth remembering that we are ultimately animals, and that the purpose of all animal life, and all life, is survival and reproduction. For many people, the drive to reproduce is an irreducible given that is impervious to argument and deliberation. The 20th century Norwegian philosopher Peter Wessel Zapffe argued, essentially, that the human capacity for reason and self-awareness breaks with nature, giving us more than we, as a part of nature, can carry. So as not to go mad, 'most people learn to save themselves by artificially limiting the content of consciousness.'

The novelist George Eliot made a similar point in her novel *Middlemarch* (1871–72):

> *That element of tragedy which lies in the very fact of frequency, has not yet wrought itself into the coarse emotion of mankind; and perhaps our frames could hardly bear much of it. If we had a keen vision and feeling of all ordinary human life, it would be like hearing the grass grow and the squirrel's heart beat, and we should die of that roar which lies on the other side of silence. As it is, the quickest of us walk about well wadded with stupidity.*

There remains a lot of social pressure on both women and men, but especially women, to have children. This social pressure may be experienced first and foremost as parental expectation, even if it remains largely silent and unspoken. But even without any social pressure, a lot of people would still choose to have children. If anything, it is a romantic idea. A friend once told me that he loved his partner so much that he wanted to mingle his genetic material with hers and live alongside what that would look like. Beyond the romance, children can fill our lives with meaning, purpose, and activity. They can remove us from our adult preoccupations into the simpler, more immediate, and more innocent dimension of our own childhood, which we are able to relive through them. The creation of another human being is almost God-like, and their need for us, at least in the early years, can give us a God-like sense of power and significance. We imagine, or hope, that they will grow up to be dutiful, that they will become our pride and solace, and that they will imitate and flatter us by having children of their own. When we die, they will say some fine words at our funeral and visit our grave. They will carry forth our name, our history, even our traits and habits, our manners and recipes. They will inherit our accumulated estate, protecting it from dispersion and dilapidation. They will prolong our work and advocate for our memory.

But having a child is not just about us. It is, we tell ourselves, an act of generosity, a gift to the world. But is that really so? More and more people are taking an opposing view. The world population stands at around 7.5 billion people, and is still rising at an annual rate of over 1%. For every person alive in Britain or America, how many animals suffer or die? How much carbon dioxide is emitted? And how much waste produced? Putting aside animal exploitation and extinction and other forms of environmental degradation, many experts are alarmed about climate change and its impact on future generations. We may go to great lengths to reduce our carbon footprint, but no amount of restraint and recycling could ever make up for the carbon footprint of bringing yet another person into the world. Rather than adding to the problem, we hope that our child will grow up to become a part of the solution. Perhaps we could offset his or her carbon footprint through environmental action, for example, by sponsoring the planting of trees. At the very least, advances in public policy and improvements in technology are likely to mitigate the impact of a rising population.

Even if having a child does contribute to the greater good, we might make an even bigger contribution by adopting an already existing child, or by remaining childless so as to concentrate all our resources on making a difference. In the *Symposium*, Plato says that animals enter into a state of love because they seek to reproduce and thereby to secure a species of immortality. Human beings, he explains, also seek to become immortal, and are prepared to take great risks, even to die, to attain fame and honour. Some people are pregnant in body and beget children to preserve their memory; but others are pregnant in soul and choose instead to beget wisdom and virtue. As their children are more beautiful and more immortal, people who are pregnant in soul have more to share with one another and a stronger bond of friendship between them. Everyone, says Plato, would rather have their children than human ones:

> *Who when he thinks of Homer and Hesiod and other great poets, would not rather have their children than ordinary ones? Who would not emulate them in the creation of children such as theirs, which have preserved their memory and given them everlasting glory?*

Plato thereby distinguishes between the lesser immortality of leaving behind children and grandchildren, which is relatively easy to achieve but only preserves our memory for at most three or four generations; and the greater immortality of leaving behind a significant artistic, intellectual, or social legacy, which is more enduring but also harder to achieve. The childless Plato wrote the *Symposium* some 2,400 years ago, and here we are today still quoting from it.

Greater immortality may not be in our grasp, but there are, of course, other reasons for remaining childless. Some people do not feel that they will make good enough parents, if only because they have no affinity for children. Others, quite simply, have not found a suitable partner, or one that they are willing to put up with for years to come. Contrary to popular belief, relationships tend to suffer from the arrival of a child, and those who have found a partner may wish to protect or enjoy their relationship by remaining childfree. In addition, many people fear that childbearing may be too traumatic or inconveniencing, or that it might damage their health or physique. They might already be in poor health, or they might be carrying a genetic disorder and worry about passing it on.

And then there are the costs involved. According to the Center for Economic and Business Research, in 2016, the cost of raising a child from birth to 21-years-old jumped to over £230,000, including more than £70,000 for childcare and babysitting alone. This figure is for a child attending state school; for a child at boarding school, it rises to just short of £500,000. To put this into perspective, in January 2017, the average value of a property in the U.K. stood at £218,255 on the House Price Index. As well as financial costs, there are opportunity costs. We swap friends, free time, restorative lie-ins, sleek interior décor, romantic evenings, and spontaneous travel for dirty diapers, temper tantrums, broken sleep, broken things, babysitting, and school runs—perhaps only to end up with a miserable or obnoxious teen on our hands. What if, deep inside, we don't even love them?

Having a child may well be good for us. It might even be good for the world. But is it actually good for the child itself? For Immanuel Kant, people, by virtue of being people, ought never to be treated as means to an end, but only ever as ends-in-themselves. If we are going to bring a child into the world, our first thought should be, not for our own good or the greater good, but for the good of the child itself. As we cannot ask a child that does not yet exist for its opinion or consent, we are left to make that decision on its behalf—and to live with the consequences for the rest of our lives. If we can see that a child would lead a miserable life, we may feel a moral obligation not to bring it into the world. But if we could be sure that it would lead a fulfilled life—which, of course, we can't— we would not feel a moral obligation to bring it into the world. In other words, we tend to place more value on the prevention of suffering than on the maximization of happiness. Most people report being satisfied with their lives. Even so, do our lives contain more suffering than happiness? Does life in general contain more suffering than happiness? On some levels, this boils down to asking whether life is preferable to death, or, at least, to non-existence.

In one of his Theban plays, *Oedipus at Colonus*, the Ancient Greek tragedian Sophocles has the chorus sing:

> *Not to be born is, beyond all estimation, best; but when a man has seen the light of day, this is next best by far, that with utmost speed he should go back from where he came.*

One of the most famous of the lost writings of Aristotle is *Eudemus,* or *On the Soul,* written in the form of a Socratic dialogue. A fragment preserved in Plutarch contains the essence of what later philosophers came to call the Wisdom of Silenus (Silenus being the tutor of Dionysus):

> *You, most blessed and happiest among humans, may well consider those blessed and happiest who have departed this life before you... This thought is indeed so old that the one who first uttered it is no longer known; it has been passed down to us from eternity, and hence doubtless it is true. Moreover, you know what is so often said and passes for a trite expression. What is that, he asked? He answered: It is best not to be born at all; and next to that, it is better to die than to live, and this is confirmed even by divine testimony ... Midas, after hunting, asked his captive Silenus somewhat urgently, what was the most desirable thing among humankind ... At length, when Midas would not stop plaguing him, he erupted with these words, though very unwillingly: "you, seed of an evil genius and precarious offspring of hard fortune, whose life is but for a day, why do you compel me to tell you those things of which it is better you should remain ignorant? For he lives with the least worry who knows not his misfortune; but for humans, the best for them is not to be born at all, not to partake of nature's excellence; not to be is best, for both sexes. This should be our choice, if choice we have; and next to this is, when we are born, to die as soon as we can." It is plain therefore, that he declared the condition of the dead to be better than that of the living.*

Arthur Schopenhauer shared in this ancient 'wisdom'. For Schopenhauer, beneath the world as it appears is the world as it actually is (Chapter 13). This is the world of will, an unconscious force that drives through all of nature, including our bodies and even our supposedly autonomous higher faculties. Although able to perceive, reason, and judge, our intellect is not designed to pierce through the veil of illusion and apprehend the true nature of reality. Instead, it and we are swept away by blind and restless will into a life of endless strife and frustration:

> *Awakened to life out of the night of unconsciousness, the will finds itself an individual, in an endless and boundless world, among innumerable individuals, all striving, suffering, erring; and as if through a troubled dream it hurries back to its old unconsciousness. Yet till then its desires are limitless, its claims inexhaustible, and every satisfied desire gives rise to a new one. No possible satisfaction in the world could suffice to still its longings, set a goal to its infinite cravings, and fill the bottomless abyss of its heart. Then let one consider what as a rule are the satisfactions of any kind that a man obtains. For the most part nothing more than the bare maintenance of this existence itself, extorted day by day with unceasing trouble and constant care in the conflict with want, and with death in prospect...*

The will is the cause of constant suffering, creating deficiencies for us to satisfy. On this account, satisfaction or happiness is not a positive state but merely the removal of striving and suffering. Once a deficiency is satisfied, another inevitably arises, and, with it, more striving and suffering. Even if satisfaction can be sustained for a short while, boredom is bound to set in. All considered, says Schopenhauer, it would have been better if we and the world had never existed. The only possible liberation comes from holding on to the realization, which is the height of Eastern spirituality, that our individuality and the world of appearances are but illusions, renounce these illusions, and wait peacefully for the eventual but ineluctable release of death.

For my part, I think that Schopenhauer is being too pessimistic, and too binary. It is possible to relish striving, or, at least, some forms of striving—like striving to make a difference, or striving to become a better person. It is also possible to rise above suffering, to grow from it, to sublime it into something bigger than ourselves. Even if life is more suffering than satisfaction—and our subjective report suggests that, for most of us, it isn't—it can still be worthwhile, and maybe more so than a hypothetical lifetime of sheer satisfaction. Life is not merely the balance of our suffering and satisfaction, but a journey of turning suffering into satisfaction, which might be called poetry, and which is the greatest happiness of all.

33

The gay revolution

Attitudes to homosexuality have undergone nothing short of a revolution in the past five decades.

First published in 1968, DSM-II (the American classification of mental disorders) actually listed homosexuality as a mental disorder. In this, the DSM followed in a long tradition in medicine and psychiatry, which in the 19th century appropriated homosexuality from the Church and, in an élan of enlightenment, transformed it from sin to mental disorder.

In those days, some therapists employed aversion therapy of the kind featured in *A Clockwork Orange* to 'cure' male homosexuality. This typically involved showing 'patients' pictures of naked men while giving them electric shocks or emetics (drugs to make them vomit), and, once they could no longer bear it, showing them pictures of naked women or sending them out on a 'date' with a young female nurse.

In 1973, the American Psychiatric Association asked all members attending its convention to vote on whether they believed homosexuality to be a mental disorder. 5,854 psychiatrists voted to remove homosexuality from the DSM, and 3,810 to retain it. The APA then compromised, removing homosexuality from the DSM but replacing it, in effect, with 'sexual orientation disturbance' for people 'in conflict with' their sexual orientation. Not until 1987 did homosexuality completely fall out of the DSM.

Meanwhile, the World Health Organization only removed homosexuality from the ICD (the international classification of mental disorders) with the publication of ICD-10 in 1992, although ICD-10 still carries the construct of 'ego-dystonic sexual orientation'. In this 'condition', the person is not in doubt about his or her sexual preference, but 'wishes it were different because of associated psychological and behavioural disorders'.

As I discuss in *The Meaning of Madness*, the evolution of the status of homosexuality in the classifications of mental disorder highlights that concepts of mental disorder can be rapidly evolving constructs that change as society changes. In 1989, Denmark became the first country to offer legal recognition for same-sex couples, and in 2001 the Netherlands became the first country to legalize same-sex marriage. On 12 March 2015, the European Parliament passed a resolution (by 472 to 115 votes) encouraging E.U. institutions and Member States to 'further contribute to reflection on the recognition of same-sex marriage or same-sex civil union as a political, social and human and civil rights issue.'

In most of the U.K. civil partnerships have been available to same-sex couples since 2005, and marriage since 13 March 2014. In the U.S. Vermont became the first state to legalize civil unions in 2000, and Massachusetts the first state to legalize same-sex marriage in 2004. On 26 June 2013, the U.S. Supreme Court ruled against the Defence of Marriage Act, which barred federal recognition of same-sex marriage. Two years later on the same day, it ruled against state level bans on same-sex marriage, thereby legalizing same-sex marriage right across the country. According to Pew Research Center polling, in 2001, 57 per cent of Americans opposed gay marriage and 35 per cent supported it; by 2017, 63 per cent supported it and only 32 per cent opposed it.

As I write, same-sex marriage is legal in the United States, Canada, the United Kingdom (with the exception of Northern Ireland), many European countries, many Latin American countries, New Zealand, and South Africa. Many other territories including Australia, Israel, and Japan offer an alternative form of recognition such as a civil union, registered partnership, or other similar construct.

At the same time, same-sex sexual relations, let alone marriage, remain illegal in many parts of Africa, the Middle East, the Caribbean, and Central, South, and Southeast Asia, in some cases punishable with life imprisonment or even death (Chapter 4). In some countries, most notably Russia and China, same-sex sexual relations are legal, but lesbian, gay, bisexual, and transgender people face substantial legal and social challenges.

Many people still think of same-sex marriage as a historical first, but this is far from being the case. Same-sex marriage was practised and accepted among precolonial peoples such as the two-spirits, the *fa'afafine*, and more than thirty African cultures; in Ancient Mesopotamia and perhaps also Ancient Egypt (Chapter 6); and in Fujian province during the Ming dynasty.

In Ancient Rome, same-sex marriage, after three centuries on the trot, was explicitly outlawed in 342 AD by the Christian co-emperors Constantius II and Constans—and it is worth noting that its return in our age corresponds with an ebbing of Christianity from the West.

In Ancient Athens, aristocratic men such as Agathon and Pausanias, who feature in Plato's *Symposium*, went beyond the pederastic tradition of mentoring young males by forming lifelong partnerships. The ancient epigram *Lovers' Lips* had for a long time been atrributed to Plato himself: 'Kissing Agathon, I had my soul upon my lips; for it rose, poor wretch, as though to cross over.'

But if there was just one thing missing from Athens and Rome, then that thing was gender parity.

34

A feminist critique of marriage

Human societies tend to various degrees of patriarchy, in which men hold primary power. Most anthropologists agree that there are no known unambiguously matriarchal societies. In the state of nature, man subjugated woman by being physically stronger, while woman was frequently incapacitated by pregnancy and childrearing, which, through giving birth and breastfeeding, naturally fell upon her. In a modern society such as ours, with technology such as mechanization and birth control, the male advantage has become largely if not entirely redundant. But still the patriarchy perdures, upheld by hoary ideology and vested interests.

This ideology is manifest, among others, in the socialization of children, which emphasizes man as breadwinner and decision-taker, and woman as mother and homemaker. Boys are encouraged to be brave and strong, while girls are expected to be passive and pretty, through, among others, fairy tales, dolls, activities such as dressing up or baking, and, above all, the examples and attitudes of role models, including historical figures. From a young age, girls in particular are indoctrinated into the virtues of marriage, which itself contributes to maintaining the traditional gender roles.

Beyond a certain age, a man who remains unmarried is thought
of as independent or intelligent, whereas a woman who remains
unmarried is assumed to be desperate, at once a figure of pity and
scorn. An unmarried man is called a bachelor—and you might
even find him on a list of eligible bachelors—but apart from the
antiquated 'maiden' or 'spinster', there is, despite the renowned
richness of the English language, no polite term for an unmarried
woman. A woman who is strong-minded enough to forgo marriage
and live out her own life is constantly made to doubt her resolve:
"Never say never… You just need to find the right man… There's
this great guy I'd like you to meet…"

On the marriage market, women are made to feel like low value,
perishable goods. To find a taker, whether for marriage or just
for sex, they need, much more than men, to conform to sexist,
ageist, and racist stereotypes, and do appalling things such as wear
makeup and high heels, which become the visible symbols of their
oppression. As they are encouraged to marry a man who is older,
more educated, and better connected, they tend to begin married
life in a doubly subordinate position, which, of course, suits the
man just fine. So much is evident from popular culture. Even
seemingly innocuous classic pop songs, which on the surface are
about romantic love, are in fact inherently sexist, revealing love
as little more than a tool of patriarchal oppression. Here, picked
almost at random, are the opening lyrics of *You Can't Hurry Love*
by the Supremes: 'I need love, love to ease my mind/ I need to
find, find someone to call mine/ But mama said you can't hurry
love/ No you just have to wait.' It would be hard to imagine these
lines in the mouth of a man. And here are the opening lyrics of
Total Eclipse of the Heart by Bonnie Tyler: 'Turnaround, every now
and then I get a little bit lonely/ And you're never coming round/

Turnaround, every now and then I get a little bit tired/ Of listening to the sound of my tears/ Turnaround, every now and then I get a little bit nervous/ That the best of all the years have gone by/ Turnaround, every now and then I get a little bit terrified/ And then I see the look in your eyes/ Turnaround bright eyes, but every now and then I fall apart.' For contrast, compare these lyrics from Chris Brown's *Fine China*: 'It's alright/ I'm not dangerous/ When you're mine/ I'll be generous/ You're irreplaceable, a collectible/ Just like fine china.'

The marriage ceremony (Chapter 26) itself is sexist beyond parody. The bride appears in a fussy white dress that symbolizes her virtue and virginity, and everyone keeps on remarking on how thin and beautiful she looks. Her father walks her down the aisle to 'give her away', and she passes, like property, from one man to another. The minister, who is traditionally a man, gives the man permission to kiss the woman, as if that is in the minister's authority and the woman has none. The man kisses, the woman is kissed. At the reception, only men are given to speak, while the bride remains seated and silent. Henceforth, the woman will adopt the man's name, as will their eventual offspring. Despite all this, the wedding day is said to belong to the woman. This, would you believe, is 'her day'.

Why should two people who want to celebrate their love and live together put themselves through a wedding, or even get married at all? Or to turn the question round, what is the state, arm in arm with the Church, doing by sanctioning the private relationships of citizens? By legitimizing a particular kind of relationship and denying others, the state is entrenching monogamy and patriarchy while devaluing and disenfranchising other forms of life and the people who choose or are forced into them, including single people, people in open or polyamorous relationships, and groups such as African Americans and the poor who for various reasons are less likely to marry. Anti-miscegenation laws that criminalized inter-racial marriages, and sometimes even inter-racial sex, remained in force in many U.S. states until as late as 1967. Is this not the state telling us who is and isn't fit to raise a family, and what that family ought to look like? Marital status is not merely a matter of social prestige, but is attached to myriad benefits in areas as diverse as banking, taxation, healthcare, and immigration.

In addition, marriage benefits the economy by producing new workers and consumers, largely through the unpaid work of women, and by making it difficult for workers with families to support to withdraw their labour. A wedding alone generates spending of, on average, £24,000 (~$32,000), and probably that again on the gift list and the travel and other expenses of the wedding guests. As much as that is, it pales into insignificance next to the £230,000+ required to raise a child, let alone two or three.

The laws that govern marriage are drafted by the state rather than the couple that has to abide by them, and while marriage is deceptively simple and straightforward to enter, it is, like the Hotel California, much more difficult to leave—and in two-thirds of cases, it is the woman who files for divorce. Divorce is a personal tragedy unnecessarily inflicted by the state on about 40% of the marriages that it sanctions, amounting in the U.S. alone to one divorce approximately every 36 seconds. When a couple divorces, people usually ask what went wrong with their marriage, without ever questioning whether there is anything wrong with marriage itself. Here are the closing lyrics of *Hotel California*: 'Mirrors on

the ceiling/ The pink champagne on ice/ And she said, 'we are all
just prisoners here, of our own device' … Last thing I remember,
I was/ Running for the door/ I had to find the passage back
to the place I was before/ 'Relax' said the night man/ 'We are
programmed to receive/ You can check out any time you like/ But
you can never leave!'"

To partake in the institution of marriage in the 21st century is also
to condone the historical abuses perpetrated in its name. Until
relatively recently, women faced a 'choice' between marriage and
a life of poverty and stigma. In many parts of the world, they
still do. In *Marriage and Morals* (1929), the philosopher Bertrand
Russell wrote that 'marriage is for woman the commonest mode
of livelihood, and the total amount of undesired sex endured by
women is probably greater in marriage than in prostitution.' Once
married, a woman's legal rights were subsumed under those of
her husband, and the so-called marriage bar restricted her ability
to work outside the home. Her husband could rape her with
impunity, and yet contraception, abortion, and divorce were all
denied to her. The rape of an unmarried woman was construed as
a property crime against her father, robbing him of his daughter's
precious virginity—with, in some cases, the woman forced to
marry her rapist. Rape of a married woman by a man other than
her husband was construed as a crime against the husband, with
little concern or regard for the woman herself. Only from the mid
20th century did evolving social norms lead to the criminalization
of marital rape, but there are still many jurisdictions in which
it remains a private matter or in which the law is not enforced.
Forced marriage is still practised the world over, including, albeit
illegally, in the U.K. and U.S., and if marriage does not require
consent, then, following that particular logic, neither does any

subsequent sexual intercourse. Many married women cannot even leave the home without their husband's permission. Women who protest or try to escape or so much as talk to another man risk being beaten or even murdered in an 'honour killing'. In 2013, an eight-year old Yemeni girl died from internal bleeding after being raped by her forty-year-old husband on 'their' wedding night.

When I was a child, it was customary for a woman to sit in the passenger seat when there was a man in the car, or in a back seat if there were two men, because everyone assumed that the man or men had to be in charge. Things have improved since then: women have much more economic and political clout than they did just twenty or thirty years ago, and men are much more egalitarian in their approach to matrimony. But women still shoulder the bulk of the housekeeping and childrearing, even when working full-time. A married man is likely to pursue his career as though he were still single, while a married woman is expected to forfeit her public life to follow her husband or care for the young, the old, and the infirm of the family. Employers look favourably upon married men, who are deemed to be more mature and responsible, while married women may be passed over for fear that they will go off to have babies or, worse, refuse to collude with the patriarchy. A vicious circle sets in. Because the man brings in more money, his time is valued and prioritized, while the woman's unpaid contributions, which she fits around the man, remain largely invisible. The more the man earns, the more the woman can afford to slip into subordination, with the middle classes leveraging their privilege to entrench the old gender stereotypes.

The truth of the matter is that a lot of people tie the knot because they are terrified of loneliness, or buckle under the social and psychological pressure that bears upon the unmarried state. But in the longer term, marriage can be even lonelier than its alternatives, and that's before it breaks up (Chapter 22). 'The trouble' said Charlotte Brontë in a letter to her correspondent (1852) 'is not that I am single and likely to stay single, but that I am lonely and likely to stay lonely.' There is also an argument that marriage is detrimental to community, weakening ties with relatives, friends, and neighbours. 'Families, I hate you!' wrote André Gide in *Les Nourritures Terrestres* (1897), 'bolted homes, shut doors, jealous repositories of happiness.' (*Familles, je vous hais! foyers clos; portes refermées; possessions jalousies du bonheur.*) There is of course the intimate relationship with the spouse, but sex can lose its appeal when it becomes a habit, or when it is taken for granted— wherefore the proliferation of sex manuals aimed at married women. In the spring of its rapture, romantic love (Chapters 13 & 14) seems to enclose the germs of freedom and fulfilment, but, with the turning of the seasons, yields nothing but failure and frustration—and it is worth remembering that man had no time for romantic love back in the day when woman was his possession.

The gay rights movement fought long and hard for gay marriage, and, in many countries, carries on the fight (Chapter 33). But ironically, this obscured the feminist message by making marriage seem like the crowning glory of love and a fundamental human right. David Cameron as *Pater Patriae* (a Roman honorific meaning 'Father of the Fatherland') declared that he supported gay marriage because he was a conservative, not in spite of it: and marriage, even gay marriage, or especially gay marriage, is a deeply conservative institution. Equality in marriage as in everything is of course to be welcome, but equality in this case should not be confused with liberation. To have the right to do something because others have it is one thing, to exercise that right is quite another. In the *Second Sex* (1949), the philosopher Simone de Beauvoir wrote that 'marriage is obscene in principle insofar as it transforms into rights and duties those mutual relations which should be founded on a spontaneous urge'. At a time of unparalleled social freedom, why, say many feminists, should we limit ourselves to an inauthentic, monotonous, and potentially calamitous life of state-enforced monogamy? Are we really so brainwashed, and so cowered, that we cannot imagine a better way of living?

Dear reader,

I hope that you enjoyed this book, and that it has supported your thinking about marriage and relationships.

I'd like to know more about you and how you got on, so feel free to drop me a line. I'll do my best to reply—although, of course, I'm unable to give marriage or other professional advice through the Internet.

I'm terrible at promoting my work, and would be tremendously grateful for any help that you could provide in bringing it to the attention of other interested readers. Please consider leaving a review on Amazon or discussing the book on your social media.

All the best,

Neel

Email: neel@neelburton.com
Facebook: @NeelBurton
Twitter: @NeelBurton

By the same author

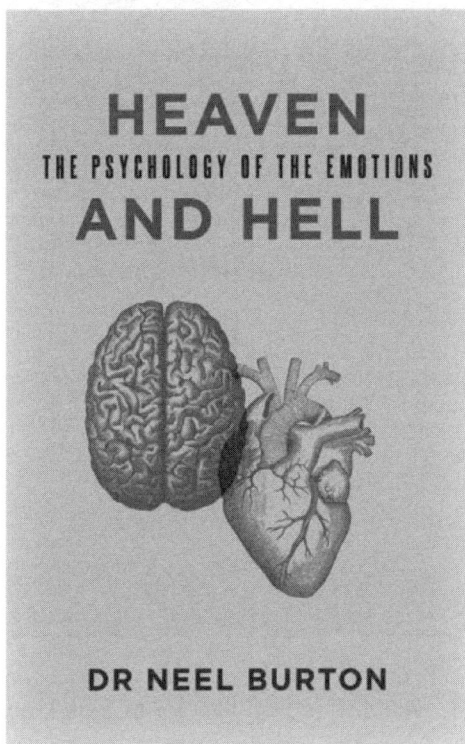

Heaven and Hell: The Psychology of the Emotions
ISBN 978-0-9929127-2-7

Many people lumber through life without giving full consideration to their emotions, partly because our empirical, materialistic culture does not encourage it or even make it seem possible, and partly because it requires unusual strength to gaze into the abyss of our deepest drives, needs, and fears. This book proposes to do just that, examining over 25 emotions ranging from lust to love and humility to humiliation, and drawing some powerful and astonishing conclusions along the way.

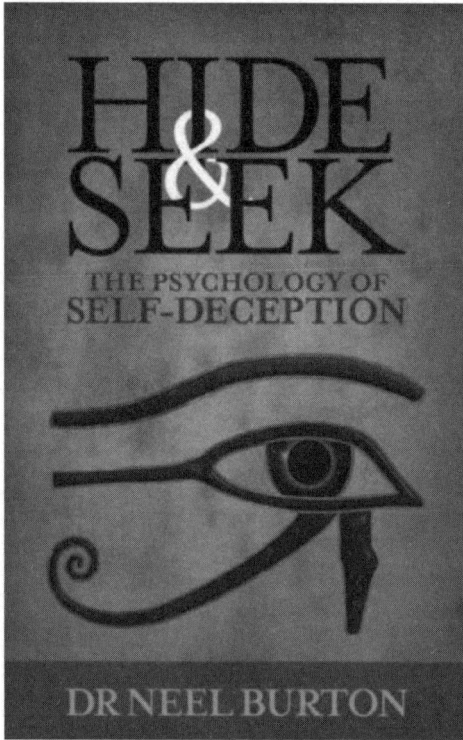

Hide and Seek: The Psychology of Self-Deception
ISBN 978-0-9560353-6-3

Self-deception is common and universal, and the cause of most human tragedies. Of course, the science of self-deception can help us to live better and get more out of life. But it can also cast a murky light on human nature and the human condition, for example, on such exclusively human phenomena as anger, depression, fear, pity, pride, dream making, love making, and god making, not to forget age-old philosophical problems such as selfhood, virtue, happiness, and the good life. Nothing could possibly be more important.

WINNER OF THE BMA YOUNG AUTHORS' AWARD

THE MEANING
OF MADNESS

SECOND EDITION

DR NEEL BURTON

The Meaning of Madness
ISBN 978-0-9929127-3-4

This book aims to open up the debate on mental disorders, to get people interested and talking, and to get them thinking. For example, what is schizophrenia? Why is it so common? Why does it affect human beings but not other animals? What might this tell us about our mind and body, language and creativity, music and religion? What are the boundaries between mental disorder and 'normality'? Is there a relationship between mental disorder and genius? These are some of the difficult but important questions that this book confronts, with the overarching aim of exploring what mental disorders can teach us about human nature and the human condition.

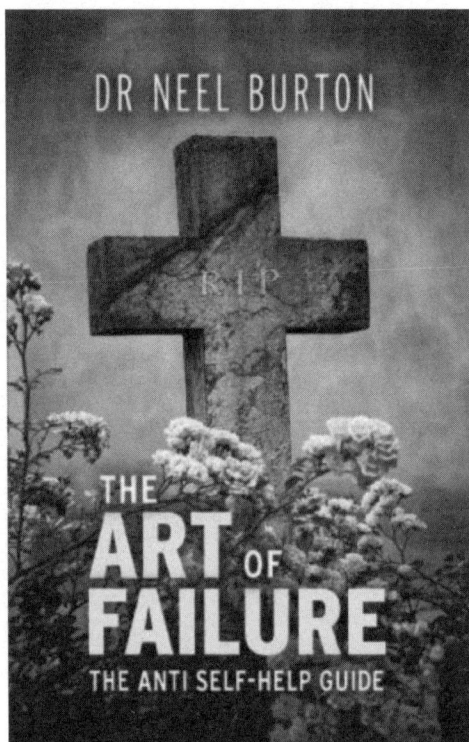

The Art of Failure: The Anti Self-Help Guide
ISBN 978-0-9560353-3-2

We spend most of our time and energy chasing success, such that we have little left over for thinking and feeling, being and relating. As a result, we fail in the deepest possible way. We fail as human beings.

The Art of Failure explores what it means to be successful, and how, if at all, true success can be achieved.

Notes

Epigraph
– Kierkegaard S. (1843): *Either/Or*. Trans. David F Swenson &
Lillian Marvin Swenson.

Chapter 1: Monogamy
– Dupanloup I et al. (2003): *A recent shift from polygyny to monogamy
in humans is suggested by the analysis of worldwide Y-chromosome
diversity*. J Mol Evol. 57(1):85–97.
– Larmuseau MH et al. (2016): *Cuckolded fathers rare in human
populations*. Trends Ecol Evol 31(5):327–9.
– Bible, *1 Kings 11:3–4 (KJV)*.
– Bible, *Deuteronomy 21:15–16 (KJV)*.
– Bible, *Genesis 1:27 (KJV)*.
– Bible, *Genesis 1:28 (KJV)*.
– Bible, *Genesis 2:18 (KJV)*.
– Bible, *Genesis 2:23 (KJV)*.
– Bible, *Genesis 2:24 (KJV)*.

Chapter 4: Gender variation and same-sex relations in precolonial peoples
– Beaglehole, JC (1967): *The Journals of Captain James Cook*.
Stanford University Press.

– Purchas, S (1905 [1625]): *Hakluytus posthumus or Purchas, his Pilgrimes*, Vol. VI. James MacLehose.
– Purchas, S (1613): *Purchas: His pilgrims…* William Stansby for Henrie Featherstone.
– Politi D. (2013): *Zimbabwe President Robert Mugabe Vows to Behead Gays*. Slate.com, 28 July 2013.
– Bolton D (2015): *Gambian President Yahya Jammeh threatens to 'slit the throats' of gay people*. Independent.co.uk, 12 May 2015.
– Smith, D (2015): *Barack Obama tells African states to abandon anti-gay discrimination*. Theguardian.com, 25 July 2015.

Chapter 5: Marriage in Ancient Egypt
– Bible, *Exodus 1:22 (KJV)*.
– Bible, *Exodus 2 (KJV)*.
– Diogenes Laertes, *Lives of Eminent Philosophers I*.
– Plutarch, *Life of Solon*.

Chapter 6: Three tales of same-sex love in Ancient Egypt
– Griffiths JG (1960): *The Conflict of Horus and Seth…* Liverpool University Press.
– Suetonius, *De vita Caesarum, Divus Julius*.
– *Papyrus Chassinat I* [P. Louvre E 25351].

Chapter 7: The history and psychology of the orgy
– Nietzsche F (1871): *The Birth of Tragedy*. Trans. Ian Johnston.
– Livy, *History of Rome* 39.18.
– For example, Lapin T (2017): *Vatican cops bust drug-fueled gay orgy at home of cardinal's aide*. Nypost.com, 5 July 2017.
– Stubbes P (1583): *The Anatomie of Abuses*, p107.
– Einstein A, as quoted in Barker P and Shugart CG (1981): *After Einstein: Proceedings of the Einstein Centennial Celebration*, p179. Memphis State University Press.

Chapter 8: Marriage in the Bible
– Bible, *1 Corinthians 7 (KJV).*
– Bible, *Ecclesiastes 7:25–26 (KJV).*
– St John Chrysostom, *Homily 19 on First Corinthians.*
– St Cyprian, *Of the Discipline and Advantage of Chastity.*
– St Augustine, *On the Good of Marriage.*
– Bible, *Genesis 24:2–4 (KJV).*
– Bible, *Deuteronomy 22:21 (KJV).*
– Bible, *Genesis 2:18.*
– Bible, *Peter 3:6 (KJV).*
– Bible, *Ephesians 5:22–24 (KJV).*
– Bible, *1 Corinthians 11:3 (KJV).*
– Bible, *Galatians 3:25-28 (KJV).*
– Bible, *1 Thessalonians 4:3–5 (KJV).*
– Bible, *Proverbs 5:18–19 (KJV).*
– Bible, *1 Corinthians 7:3–4 (KJV).*
– Bible, *Deuteronomy 25:5–6 (KJV).*
– Bible, *Genesis 38 (KJV).*
– Bible, *Matthew 5:28 (KJV).*
– Bible, *Deuteronomy 23:2 (KJV).*
– Bible, *Matthew 5:32 (KJV), and echoed in Mark and Luke.*
– Bible, *Matthew 19:4–6 (KJV).*

Chapter 9: Love in the Bible
– Bible, *1 Corinthians 13 (NRSV).*
– Bible, *1 Corinthians 13:13 (KJV).*
– Bible, *Solomon 2:1–3 (KJV).*
– Bible, *1 Samuel 18 (KJV).*
– Bible, *1 Samuel 20:30 (KJV).*
– Bible, *2 Samuel 1:26 (KJV).*
– Bible, *Ruth 1:16 (KJV).*

– Bible, *Ruth 4:14–17 (KJV)*.

Chapter 10: Same-sex relations in the Bible
– Bible, *Leviticus 18:22 (KJV)*.
– Bible, *Leviticus 20:13 (KJV)*.
– Bible, *1 Corinthians 6:9 (KJV)*.
– Bible, *1 Timothy 1:10 (KJV)*.
– Bible, *Genesis 19:9 (KJV)*.
– Bible, *Romans 1:26–28 (KJV)*.
– Bible, *Matthew 19:12 (KJV)*.

Chapter 11: An interpretation of Adam and Eve
– Hill, JP (2014): *National Study of Religion and Human Origins*.
  Study funded by the Biologos Foundation.
– Bible, *Genesis 1:27 (KJV)*.
– Bible, *Genesis 2:16 (KJV)*.
– Plato, *Republic*.
– Bible, *Genesis 2:18 (KJV)*.
– Bible, *Genesis 2:23 (KJV)*.
– Bible, *John 1:1 (KJV)*.
– Bible, *Genesis 2:24 (KJV)*.
– Plato, *Symposium*.
– Bible, *Genesis 3:5 (KJV)*.
– Bible, *Genesis 3:7 (KJV)*.
– Bible, *Numbers 22:28 (KJV)*.
– Bible, *Proverbs 16:18 (KJV)*.
– Bible, *Isaiah 14:12–14 (KJV)*.
– Bible, *Genesis 3:12 (KJV)*.
– Bible, *Genesis 3:13 (KJV)*.
– Bible, *Genesis 3:15 (KJV)*.
– Bible, *Genesis 3:19 (KJV)*.

– Bible, *Genesis 3:22 (KJV)*.
– Bible, *Genesis 5:5 (KJV)*.
– Tertullian, *On the Apparel of Women I*.
– Hugo V. (1856): *Les Contemplations*.

Chapter 12: Sex, sexuality, and duplicity in Ancient Rome
– Tacitus, *Annals XIV*. Trans. Neel Burton.
– Suetonius, *De vita Caesarum, Divus Augustus para. 65*. Trans. Robert Graves.
– Livy, *History of Rome*.
– Musonius Rufus, *On Sexual Indulgence*.
– Polybius, *Histories VI*.
– Gibbon E (1776–1788): *The Decline and Fall of the Roman Empire Vol I, ch. 2, footnote 31*.
– Martial, *Epigrams XI:XLIII*.
– Seneca, *On the Happy Life VII*.

Chapter 13: How love became the new religion
– John Butler Trio: *Fool for You*. In *April Uprising* (2010). John Charles Wiltshire-Butler for Because Music.
– Arnold M (1852): *Empedocles on Etna*.
– Sophocles, *Antigone*. Trans. Robert Fagles.
– Plato, *Symposium*. Trans. Benjamin Jowett.
– Aristotle, *Nicomachen Ethics VIII*. Trans. WD Ross.
– Montaigne M, *On Friendship*. Trans. Donald Frame.
– Boétie E, as quoted in Bakewell S (2011): *A life of Montaigne…* p92. Vintage Books.
– Ovid, *The Heroines*. Trans. G Showerman.
– Ovid, *The Art of Love II*. Trans. J Lewis May.
– Schopenhauer A (1819), *The World as Will and Representation*.
– Bible: *Genesis 22:12 (KJV)*.

– Bible: *John 3:14–15 (KJV)*.
– Bible: *Matthew 5:44 (KJV)*.
– St Francis of Assisi, *Canticle of the Creatures*. Trans. Franciscan Friars Third Order Regular.
– Spinoza, Baruch (1677): *Ethics I, 15 & 18*.

Chapter 14: The psychology of romantic love
– Cervantes M (1615): *Don Quixote 1.13*.
– St Augustine, *Confessions*.
– Lewis, CS (1955): *Surprised by Joy*.
– Lewis, CS (1941): *The Weight of Glory*.

Chapter 15: The history of kissing
– Vātsyāyana, *Kama Sutra II, 3: On Kissing*.
– Homer, *Iliad XXIV*. Trans. Samuel Butler.
– Herodotus, *Histories I, 134*.
– Herodotus, *An Account of Egypt*.
– Bible, *Solomon 1:2 (KJV)*.
– Catullus, *Catullus VIII*. Trans. AS Kline.
– Bible, *Luke 22:48 (KJV)*.

Chapter 16: Who was Valentine?
– Chaucer G (1382): *Parlement of Foules*.
– Charles d'Orléans (1416): *Rondeau to his wife, Bonne d'Armagnac*.
– Shakespeare W (1602): *Hamlet IV, 5*.
– Rahim Z (2017): *Here's how much people are expected to spend on Valentine's Day*. Fortune.com, 7 February 2017.

Chapter 17: The 7 types of love
– Flaubert G (1856): *Madame Bovary*. Trans. Alan Russell.
– Lee JA (1973): *Colours of Love*. New Press.

- Aristotle, *Nicomachean Ethics X.*
- Plato, *Lysis.*
- Plato, *Phaedrus.*
- Plato, *Symposium.*

Chapter 18: Polyamory: A new way of loving?
- Shelley, PB (1821): *Epipsychidion.*

Chapter 19: The philosophy of lust
- Bible, *1 Corinthians* 7 *(KJV).*
- Dante (1472): *Divine Comedy, Inferno V.*
- Schopenhauer A (1819): *The World as Will and Representation.*
- Bhagavad Gita 3:36–43.
- Baudelaire C, as quoted in Richardson J (1994): *Baudelaire*, p50.
- Kant I (1796): *The Philosophy of Law.* Trans. W. Hastie.
- Amis K (1963): *One Fat Englishman.* Gollancz.
- Shakespeare W (1609): *Sonnet 129.*
- Baudelaire C, as quoted in Richardson J (1994): *Baudelaire*, p50.
- Plato, *Symposium.*

Chapter 20: The magic of masturbation
- Stephens-Davidowitz S (2015): *Searching for sex.* Nytimes.com, 24 January 2015.
- Das A (2007): *Masturbation in the United States.* Journal of Sex and Marital Therapy 33:301.
- Bible, *Genesis 38:10 (KJV).*
- Stengers J & van Neck A (2001): *Masturbation: the history of a great terror*, p56–57. Palgrave.
- Kant I (1797): *Metaphysics of Morals.* Trans. James W. Ellington.
- Rousseau JJ (1762): *Emile, or On Education.* Trans. Barbara Foxley.

– Rousseau JJ (1782): *Confessions III*. Trans. JM Cohen.
– Esquirol JED (1838): *Concerning Mental Illnesses*.
– Hurlbert DF & Whittaker KE (1991): *The role of masturbation in marital and sexual satisfaction: A comparative study of female masturbators and nonmasturbators*. Journal of Sex Education and Therapy. Vol 17, issue 4.
– Gerressu M et al. (2008): *Prevalence of masturbation and associated factors in a British National Probability Survey*. Arch Sex Behav 37(2):266–278.
– Baker RR & Bellis MA (1993): *Human sperm competition: ejaculate adjustment by males and the function of masturbation*. Anim. Behav. 46:861–885.
– Giles GG et al (2003): *Sexual factors and prostate cancer*. BJU Int. 92(3):211–6.
– Baker RR & Bellis MA (1993): *Human sperm competition: ejaculate manipulation by females and a function for the female orgasm*. Anim. Behav. 46:887–909.
– Wenner M (2006): *Why do guys get sleepy after sex?* Scienceline. org, 25 September 2006.
– Davey Smith G et al. (1997): *Sex and death: are they related? Findings from the Caerphilly Cohort Study*. BMJ 315(7123):1641–1644.

Chapter 21: Touch hunger
– Collins P: *Fly in the Ointment*. Solitarywatch.com, 13 July 2015.
– Watson JB & Watson RA (1928): *Psychological Care of Infant and Child*. WW Norton & Company, Inc.
– Carlson M & Earls F (1999): *Psychological and endocrinological sequelae of early social deprivation in institutionalized children in Romania*. In Carter CS et al (eds.): *The Integrative Neurobiology of Affiliation*. MIT Press.

– Anthony J (2015): *39 percent of your coworkers masturbate at the office, according to our survey.* TimeOut New York, 21 December 2015.
– Kraus MW et al (2010): *Tactile communication, cooperation, and performance: an ethological study of the NBA.* Emotion 10(5):745–9.
– Cruso AH & Wetzel CG (1984): *The Midas touch: The effects of interpersonal touch on restaurant tipping.* Personality and Social Psychology Bulletin 10:512–517.
– Guéguen N (2004): *Nonverbal encouragement of participation in a course: the effect of touching.* Social Psychology of Education 7:89–98.
– Stephen R & Zweigenhaft R (1985): *The effect on tipping of a waitress touching male and female customers.* Journal of Social Psychology 126:141–142.
– Hornik J (1992): *Tactile stimulation and consumer response.* Journal of Consumer Research 19:449–458.

Chapter 22: The pain of loneliness/the joy of solitude

– Pascal B (1670): *Pensées 139.* Trans. WF Trotter.
– Wilson T (2014): *Just think: The challenges of the disengaged mind.* Science 345(6192), 75–77.
– Siddique H (2017): *Three-quarters of older people in the UK are lonely, survey finds.* Theguardian.com, 21 March 2017.
– DePaulo B (2016): *What no one ever told you about people who are single.* Plenary address to the APA, 5 August 2016.
– Chekov A (1921): *Note-Book of Anton Chekhov.* Trans. SS Koteliansky & Leonard Woolf.
– Nietzsche F (1886): *Beyond Good and Evil 2, 49.* Trans. Helen Zimmern.
– Nietzsche F (1881): *The Dawn of Day, 491.* Trans. John McFarland Kennedy.

– Rilke RM (1902): *Letter to Paula Modersohn-Becker*, dated 12 February 1902. Trans. Jane Bannard Greene & MD Herter Norton.
– Storr A (1988): *Solitude*, p. 202. Flamingo.

Chapter 23: The ascetic alternative
– Bible, *Matthew 19:12 (KJV)*.
– Bible, *Matthew 19:22 (KJV)*.

Chapter 24: Are married people healthier?
– Robles TF et al (2014): *Marital quality and health: a meta-analytic review*. Psychol Bull 140(1):140–87.
– Hayes RM et al. (2016): *The impact of marital status on mortality and length of stay in patients admitted with acute coronary syndrome*. Int J Cardiol. 212:142–4.
– Ploubidis GB et al. (2015): *Life-course partnership status and biomarkers in midlife: Evidence from the 1958 British Birth Cohort*. Am J Public Health 105(8):1596–603.
– Wu Z et al. (2003): *In sickness and in health: Does cohabition count?* Journal of Family Issues 24:811–38.
– Levine GN et al. (2013): *Pet ownership and cardiovascular risk: a scientific statement from the American Heart Association*. Circulation 127(23):2353–63.
– Hughes ME & Waite LJ (2009): *Marital biography and health at mid-life*. J Health Soc Behav. 50(3):344–358.
– Tucker JS et al. (1996): *Marital history at midlife as a predictor of longevity: alternative explanations to the protective effect of marriage*. Health Psychol. 15(2):94–101.

Chapter 25: The deep psychology of the bachelor party
– Van Gennep, A. (1909): *Les rites de passage*.

– Kierkegaard S. (1843): *Either/Or*. Trans. David F Swenson & Lillian Marvin Swenson.

– Woolf V. (1925): *Mrs Dalloway*.

Chapter 26: Should we have a big wedding?

– Francis-Tan A & Mialon HM (2015): *'A diamond is forever' and other fairy tales: The relationship between wedding expenses and marriage duration*. Economic Inquiry 53(4):1919–1930.

Chapter 28: The philosophy of trust

– Plato, *Republic I*.

– Macchiavelli N (1532): *The Prince XXI*.

– Aristotle, *Nicomachean Ethics X*.

– Hobbes T (1651): *Leviathan I, 13*.

– Hobbes T (1651): *Leviathan II, 17*.

– Hume D (1739): *Treatise on Human Nature II, 2, 5*.

Chapter 29: The philosophy of forgiveness

– Chapman T (1988): *Baby can I hold you*. Tracy Chapman for Elektra/Asylum Records.

– Eads L (2017): *Five jailed over failed £50m Chasseuil wine heist*. Thedrinksbusiness.com, 26 June 2017.

– Tolstoy L (1869): *War and Peace*.

– Plato, *Apology*.

– Aristotle, *Nicomachean Ethics III*.

– Seneca, *On Anger*.

– Aristotle, *Rhetoric II*.

– Bible, *Leviticus 16:10 (KJV)*.

– Bible, *John 1:29 (KJV)*.

– Bible, *Psalms 103:12 (KJV)*.

– Bible, *Ephesians 4:31–32 (KJV)*.

– Bible, *Matthew 6:15 (KJV)*.

– Bible, *Luke 15:32 (KJV)*.

Chapter 30: The rise and demise of divorce

– Office for National Statistics: *Divorces in England and Wales: 2015*.

– National Center for Family and Marriage Research: *Divorce rate in the U.S.: Geographic variation, 2015*.

– Bible, *Matthew 5:32 (KJV)*. Echoed in Mark and Luke.

– Office for National Statistics: *Marriages in England and Wales: 2014*.

– Office for National Statistics: *Births in England and Wales: 2015*.

– Eurostat: *Marriage and divorce statistics*. Data extracted in June 2017.

– Benson H for the Marriage Foundation: *Keeping up with the neighbours. The influence of local wealth and faith on marriage*. May 2017.

– McPherson M et al. (2006): *Social isolation in America: Changes in Core Discussion Networks over two decades*. Sociological Review 71:353–375.

Chapter 31: The future of the family

– Office for National Statistics: *Families and households in the UK: 2016*.

– Department of Education: *Children looked after in England including adoption: 2015 to 2016*.

Chapter 32: Should we have children?

– Kirchgaessner S (2015): *Pope Francis: not having children is selfish*. Theguardian.com, 11 February 2015.

– Bible, *Psalm 127 (KJV)*.

– Bible, *Genesis 1:28 (KJV)*.

– Office for National Statistics: *Statistical Bulletin: Births in England and Wales: 2016*.

– Deaton A & Stone AA (2013): *Evaluative and hedonic wellbeing among those with and without children at home*. Proc Natl Acad Sci USA 111(4):1328–1333.

– Anderson J (2014): *The impact of family structure on the health of children: Effects of divorce*. Linacre Q. 81(4):378–387.

– Benson H for the Marriage Foundation: *Keeping up with the neighbours. The influence of local wealth and faith on marriage*. May 2017.

– Zapffe PW (1933): *The Last Messiah*.

– Zapffe PW (1941): *On the Tragic*.

– Eliot G (1871–2): *Middlemarch 20*.

– Plato, *Symposium*. Trans. Benjamin Jowett.

– Doss BD et al (2009): *The effect of the transition to parenthood on relationship quality: An 8-year prospective study*. J Pers Soc Psychol 96(3):601–619.

– Collinson P (2016): *Cost of raising children in UK higher than ever*. Theguardian.com, 16 February 2016.

– Sophocles, *Oedipus at Colonus, 1225*. Trans. Richard Jebb.

– Aristotle, *Eudemus*. Fragment quoted in Plutarch, *Moralia, Consolatio ad Apollonium*. Trans. S. H.

– Schopenhauer A (1819), *The World as Will and Representation, 46: On the vanity and suffering of life*. Trans. Haldane and Kemp.

Chapter 33: The gay revolution

– Voting numbers at the 1973 APA convention are from Davies J (2013): *Cracked: Why Psychiatry is Doing More Harm Than Good*. Icon Books.

– Love R (2015): *European parliament votes in favour of report declaring marriage equality a human right.* Attitude.co.uk, 14 March 2015.

– Masci D et al. (2017): *5 facts about same-sex marriage.* Pewresearch.org, 26 June 2017.

– *Lovers' Lips* attributed to Plato by Diogenes Laertes, *Lives of Eminent Philosophers III.*

– *Lovers' Lips* in Mackail JW (1906): *Select Epigrams from the Greek.*

Chapter 34: A feminist critique of marriage

– Supremes, The (1966): *You Can't Hurry Love.* Holland-Dozier-Holland for Motown.

– Tyler, B (1983): *Total Eclipse of the Heart.* Jim Steinman for Columbia Records.

– Brown, C (2013): *Fine China.* Chris Brown, Eric Bellinger, Leon 'Roccstar' Youngblood, and Sevyn Streeter for RCA Records.

– Brides (2016): *How much does a wedding cost?* Bridesmagazine. co.uk, 12 September 2016.

– Collinson P (2016): *Cost of raising children in UK higher than ever.* Theguardian.com, 16 February 2016.

– CDC/NCHS National Vital Statistics System: National marriage and divorce rate trends 2000–2015. Retrieved on 26 August 2017.

– Eagles, The (1977): *Hotel California.* Don Felder, Don Henley, and Glenn Frey for Asylum.

– Russell B (1929): *Marriage and Morals 11: Prostitution.*

– Elie J (2013): *Yemeni child bride, eight, 'dies on wedding night'.* Theguardian.com, 11 September 2013.

– Brontë C (1852): *Letter to Ellen Nussey dated 25 August 1852* in Smith M (2004): *The Letters of Charlotte Brontë Vol. 3.* Clarendon Press.

– Gide, A (1897): *Les Nourritures Terrestres IV.* Trans. Neel Burton.

– Guardian, The (2011): *David Cameron's Conservative party conference speech in full.* Theguardian.com, 5 October 2011.

– Beauvoir S (1949): *The Second Sex* (Vintage, 1989) *444.* Trans. HM Parshley.

Index

bisexuality, 88, 90
Bovary, Emma, 81
bridal veil, 140
bride price (see also, *dowry*), 19
bridesmaids, 140
Brontë, C, 195
Brown, C, 191
Bruno of Cologne, St, 123
Buddha, 93, 183
bungee jumping, 135

Caesar, Julius, 5, 22
California, 164
Cameron, David, 195
Cana, 35
Canossa, 158
carbon footprint, 178
cardiovascular disease, 101, 110, 129, 130
Carlson, M, 106
Carnival, 28
Carthusian Order, 123
Cassian, John, 121
Catholic Church, 3, 15, 28, 33, 38, 56, 65, 75, 77, 92, 98, 117–127, 139, 140, 160, 168, 188, 191
Catullus, 75
cave paintings, 97, 133
celibacy, 31, 32, 97, 111, 126, 127, 129, 130, 131, 143, 166, 173, 192, 195
Celtic monasticism, 121–122
cereal packet family, 170, 174
Cernunnos, 133
Cervantes, Miguel de, 69–70
charity, 38, 65, 76, 83, 127
Chartreuse, 123
chastity, 18, 31, 52, 54
Chaucer, G, 78
cheating, 87, 88

Chekov, A, 113
cherubim, 47
children, 2, 8, 11, 13, 19, 35, 52, 83, 89, 94, 106, 110, 164, 165, 166, 169, 170, 171, 172, 173, 174, 175–184, 189, 192
Cistercian Order, 123
Cîteaux, 123
civil union, 166, 186, 187
Cleopatra, 20
Climacus, John, 120
Clinton, Bill, 91
coenobitic monastery, 119
cohabitation, 130, 143, 166, 171, 172, 174, 176
Columba, 122
Columbanus, 122
concubine, 6, 53
Congo Basin, 97
Constantine, 120
contraception, 18, 34, 175, 189, 193
Cook, Captain James, 14
cortisol, 106, 130
courtly love, see *troubadours*
creation story, 3, 35, 43–49
crying of the banns, 140, 142
cuckold, 2
Cupid, 82

Dalai Lama, 131
Dante, 92, 160
dating, 148
David, 2, 34, 38–39, 40, 66, 91
David and Jonathan, 38–39
David, St, 122
decretei children, 106
Defence of Marriage Act, 187
depression, 110, 129
desire, 70–71
Diogenes the Cynic, 100